STUDIES IN
ANTHROPOLOGICAL METHOD

General Editors

GEORGE AND LOUISE SPINDLER

Stanford University

BEYOND HISTORY:
THE METHODS OF PREHISTORY

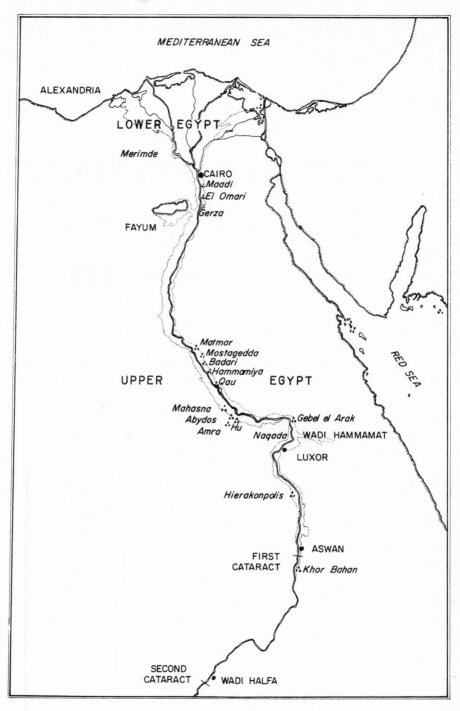

MEDITERRANEAN SEA

ALEXANDRIA

LOWER EGYPT

Merimde

CAIRO
Maadi
El Omari
Gerza

FAYUM

UPPER   EGYPT

Matmar
Mostagedda
Badari
Hammamiya
Qau

Mahasna
Abydos
Amra   Hu
Naqada   WADI HAMMAMAT

Gebel el Arak

LUXOR

Hierakonpolis

RED SEA

FIRST
CATARACT   ASWAN
Khor Bahan

SECOND
CATARACT   WADI HALFA

Map of Egypt showing the location of major Predynastic sites.

BEYOND HISTORY: THE METHODS OF PREHISTORY

BRUCE G. TRIGGER

McGill University

HOLT, RINEHART AND WINSTON

New York   Chicago   San Francisco   Atlanta

Dallas   Montreal   Toronto   London

FOREWORD

ABOUT THE SERIES

Anthropology has been, since the turn of the century, a significant influence shaping Western thought. It has brought into proper perspective the position of our culture as one of many and has challenged universalistic and absolutistic assumptions and beliefs about the proper condition of man. Anthropology has been able to make this contribution mainly through its descriptive analyses of non-Western ways of life. Only in the last decades of its comparatively short existence as a science have anthropologists developed systematic theories about human behavior in its transcultural dimensions, and only very recently have anthropological techniques of data collection and analysis become explicit and in some instances replicable.

Teachers of anthropology have been handicapped by the lack of clear, authoritative statements of how anthropologists collect and analyze relevant data. The results of fieldwork are available in many reports and they can be used to demonstrate cultural diversity and integration, social control, religious behavior, marriage customs, and the like, but clear, systematic statements about how the facts are gathered and interpreted are rare in the literature readily available to students. Without this information the alert reader of anthropological literature is left uninformed about the process of our science, knowing only of the results. This is an unsatisfying state of affairs for both the student and the instructor.

This series is designed to help solve this problem. Each study in the series focuses upon manageable dimensions of modern anthropological methodology. Each one demonstrates significant aspects of the processes of gathering, ordering, and interpreting data. Some are highly selected dimensions of methodology. Others are concerned with the whole range of experience involved in studying a total society. These studies are written by professional anthropologists who have done fieldwork and have made significant contributions to the science of man and his works. In them the authors explain how they go about this work, and to what end. We think they will be helpful to students who want to know what processes of inquiry and ordering stand behind the formal, published results of anthropology.

ABOUT THE AUTHOR

Bruce G. Trigger is currently an associate professor of anthropology at Mc-Gill University. He has a B.A. degree in anthropology from the University of Toronto and a Ph.D. in anthropology from Yale University. His principal concern is with the problems of correlating data from different fields for the study of prehistory. He has done archeological fieldwork in Ontario and later in Egypt and the Sudan. He was chief archeologist with the University of Pennsylvania–Yale University Expedition to Egypt and with the Oriental Institute Sudan Expedition. Both of these expeditions were part of the UNESCO Nubian Campaign designed to promote archeological work in the portion of the Nile Valley threatened by the construction of the High Dam at Aswan. Professor Trigger has published two books, *History and Settlement in Lower Nubia* and *The Late Nubian Settlement at Arminna West,* as well as various papers on French-Indian relations in Canada, settlement archeology and the culture history of the Sudan. He has just finished a major study of the ethnohistory of the St. Lawrence Valley in the sixteenth century.

ABOUT THE BOOK

This study has the great virtue of making the premises and analytic principles of a significant field of inquiry explicit. As Professor Trigger points out, prehistory —like its mother-discipline of history—has been oriented more toward facts than toward theory, and its methodological literature is neither as extensive nor as well formulated as that of archeology.

The author makes it clear that the prehistorian must operate with concepts and technical data from many disciplines. The processes inherent in the cultural change and sociopolitical development that the prehistorian wishes to reconstruct are not confined to any single science. Professor Trigger shows how geology, geography, linguistics, ethnology, folklore and mythology, physical anthropology, social anthropology, and other fields make direct contributions to the methods and theory as well as the technical content of the prehistorian's work. He also demonstrates how the prehistorian must examine the evidence and logic supporting the rival claims of scholars in these contributing disciplines himself, rather than accepting their conclusions without question. A climatic change, for example, that would have very signifiant implications for population movement and settlement in an area, may be presented quite differently by various geologists, but the conclusions of some will appear more reasonable than others in the light of certain evidence.

The methodology of prehistory is placed in relationship to history, to ethnology and to archeology—those disciplines most akin to prehistory. The task is defined as the reconstruction of man's cultural and social development during prehistoric times. Each of these closely related fields is seen as complementing each other, and rounding out the chronicle of man's development. The problems that prehistory sets out to solve are the same as those shared by social and cultural anthropologists: What are the components of culture and how do they interact? What are the boundaries of a culture and how do they change? What are the relationships among socio-political complexity, subsistence techniques, and environment?

Students of social and cultural anthropology will benefit from a reading of this book, for they will see these familiar problems in the perspective of time and within the framework of a wide-ranging methodology. In addition, they will be better able to discuss and evaluate the assumptions underlying site reports and general works on prehistory. Readers are aided directly in this effort not only by the general text and case analysis, but also by a very useful selected and evaluated bibliography at the end of the book.

The book is also notable for the application of the general principles enunciated to a single case, namely, Predynastic Egypt. The latter is defined as constituted of all known food-producing cultures of Egypt prior to the unification of the country around 3000 B.C. The author points out that the study of Egyptian prehistory has been handicapped by the absence of applications of methods used in the interpretation of other early civilizations. He presents evidence for cultural continuity and indigenous social and cultural development versus evidence for development from migration and diffusion, then interprets this evidence in the light of the previous general discussion. He also uses examples, within the general body of the text, from many other areas, notably Nubia and northeastern North America.

Students and instructors in anthropology, archeology, ethnology, and prehistory, as well as many in history, will find this text of unusual interest.

GEORGE AND LOUISE SPINDLER
General Editors
Stanford, February 1968

PREFACE

In recent years American archeology has been growing increasingly self-conscious. This selfconsciousness has generated a stream of methodological studies that seek to examine the basic premises of the discipline. Among the books to appear since the text of this one was completed, I cannot fail to mention Kwang-chih Chang's *Rethinking Archaeology* and James F. Deetz's *Invitation to Archaeology*.

The present study seeks to fill a curious gap in the contemporary anthropological literature. Among the monographs that have appeared so far, none has been devoted exclusively to the problems encountered in reconstructing and interpreting the history of human groups for which there are no written records. The skills needed to cope with these problems constitute the techniques of prehistory as distinguished from archeology. The aim of *Beyond History: The Methods of Prehistory* is to provide a discussion of the methodology of prehistory, a subject usually relegated to a back chapter in textbooks of prehistoric archeology.

My interest in the methodology of prehistory began when I attempted to unravel certain problems in Nubian history. This work convinced me that the reconstruction of prehistory is frequently more difficult than one would care to admit and that prehistorians rarely keep in mind the full range of alternative explanations to which their data may be susceptible. In a discipline where interpretations are fraught with uncertainty, it is important to be sophisticated about these alternatives.

A second gap that this book seeks to fill is that of a discussion of cultural development in Predynastic Egypt couched in anthropological terms. The development of civilization in Egypt had long interested me, and colleagues had been urging me to produce something along these lines. The possibility of combining these two topics appealed to me. Most of the examples that I use, when they do not concern ancient Egypt, are drawn from the two other areas that I know best, Nubia and the Northeastern Woodland region of North America.

Since this study straddles two fields—anthropology and Egyptology—it suffers of necessity from the problems that afflict mongrel works. To the prehistorian who is unfamiliar with the speculation of Egyptologists, many of the theoretical points will appear unduly labored; to the Egyptologist, on the other hand, the treatment of the substantive material may seem sparse and poorly documented. It is hoped that enough conclusions of mutual interest have emerged to justify this interdisciplinary effort. It should be remembered also that this book is intended as a text and that this has influenced our manner of presentation.

I wish to thank Professor William K. Simpson of the Department of Near Eastern Languages, Yale University, for commenting on the sections of the manuscript dealing with ancient Egypt. I wish also to thank my two part-time research assistants, Mrs. Gillian Sankoff and Mr. Roger McDonnell, who did bibliographic research and read and commented critically on the first draft of the book. Their time was made available to me by the Department of Sociology and Anthropology, McGill University. The map and illustrations were drawn by Mrs. Susan Weeks and the cost of preparing the manuscript was defrayed by a grant from the Pollack Research Fund.

B. G. TRIGGER

Montreal, Canada
February 1968

CONTENTS

BEYOND HISTORY:
THE METHODS OF PREHISTORY

Introduction

History and Archeology

ISTORY, in its most literal sense, is the study of change from earliest times down to the present. Human (as distinguished from natural) history attempts to arrange the events that have happened to mankind in chronological order and to explain them. The academic discipline called history is even more narrowly defined (Nagel 1961:547). The latter grew out of the commemoration in story and song of the deeds of the mighty, and long after it became a scholarly discipline continued to treat its subject matter largely in a biographic fashion. Most, if not all, the data that historians work with are written records and they are generally agreed that without such records there can be no true history.

Most recent history is based on records that have been passed down from generation to generation since the time they were written, but the history of earlier periods is more often based on writings which are recovered through archeological excavations. Most of our knowledge of the history of China or of classical Greece and Rome, for instance, comes from documents of the first sort and, in these cases, archeological evidence merely serves to confirm or round out known sources. The writing systems and most of the records of ancient Egypt and Mesopotamia were lost for many centuries and the reconstruction of the history of these ancient civilizations has only been possible through close cooperation between archeologists and philologists. Thus, even though many (but not all) Assyriologists and Egyptologists study these ancient civilizations through their written records, they remain dependent on archeologists for their historical materials.

Even when we take both kinds of history into account, they cover only a small number of societies and an even more limited range of types. Human development appears to have begun over two million years ago, but the earliest written records are only about 5000 years old, and in most parts of the world they are much younger. Even the Inca and Aztec civilizations, lacking developed writing systems, stand beyond the reach of true history. As a result, adequate historical documentation is available for only a small number of complex societies. In addition, there are a few more societies which either had writing, but used it for very limited purposes, or else wrote on materials that have not survived. These and the small number of nonliterate societies about which information is recorded in the literature of nearby cultures constitute the so-called proto- or parahistoric cultures (C. Hawkes 1954:159–160). Almost all of the highly developed cultures of Africa and bronze age Europe, as well as the food gathering and simpler horticultural societies throughout the world, lie outside the scope of history. These ahistorical groups are precisely the ones that anthropologists, with their traditional interest in small scale, nonliterate societies, find most interesting.

Prehistory

In the first half of the nineteenth century, when many knowledgeable people believed that the world was less than 6000 years old, there was little awareness that most of the record of man's development lay beyond the pale of written history. It was possible for a reasonable man to interpret Christian Thomsen's (1836) successive ages of stone, bronze, and iron as being applicable to Denmark, where this three-age system was developed, and yet to quote with approval a Biblical text that appeared to indicate that ironworking had been invented in the Near East seven generations after Adam. This view of human history was supported by the geology of the day, which postulated that the earth "evolved" by a series of universal catastrophies, each followed by a new creation. According to this line of reasoning, man was created only after the last general catastrophe.

Because human history was believed to have little depth in time, there was a tendency to ascribe all archeological remains to known peoples, such as the Vikings or Phoenicians. Typical of this antiquarian type of approach was the argument advanced by John Bagford, early in the eighteenth century, concerning the bones of a mammoth that were found in association with some crude stone tools near London. These, he said, were the remains of a Roman war elephant killed by the ancient Britons (Daniel 1963:49). More sceptical writers such as Samuel Johnson, argued, however, that it was in vain to speculate about ancient monuments because "we can know no more than what old writers have told us" (Daniel 1963:35).

Eventually, however, the idea of geological catastrophism began to give way to Charles Lyell's (1830–1833) theory that the forces that produced the geological formations of the past operate in the same way that geological forces do today. This opened the way for the development of Charles Darwin's monumental theory of biological evolution (1859) which in turn yielded the idea that man might have existed much longer than hitherto had been believed and that he and his culture both might be products of *gradual* as opposed to sudden creation. Geologists and archeologists now began to work together studying Pleistocene geological formations. As a result of this experience, archeologists became accustomed to grouping artifacts, or cultural finds, together according to the level from which they came and trying to work out the developmental relationships between the different levels. Out of this fruitful cooperation was born a new discipline which attempted to trace human history into the dark period before man decided to inscribe on tablets an imperfect record of his myriad thoughts and experiences.

Although the adjective *préhistorique* was used by Tournal as early as 1833 (Heizer 1962:72–83), *prehistory* was first proposed as the name of a discipline in a book entitled *The Archaeology and Prehistoric Annals of Scotland,* published by Daniel Wilson in 1851. Wilson defined prehistory as a study dealing with periods or kinds of historical data the chroniclings of which were undesigned. The term was used by Sir John Lubbock in 1865 in his book *Prehistoric Times* and thirteen years later it became accepted usage (Daniel 1963:13). Although the term has occasionally been criticized, it has the merit of stressing (perhaps in a way that Wilson's original definition does not bring out clearly) that prehistory takes up the study of man's past at the point where recorded history stops. Among English-speaking scholars, the prehistoric period is viewed as beginning in any region at the time when adequate written records cease to be available.

It should be noted that archeology is not a synonym for prehistory. Archeology is a discipline concerned with the techniques involved in recovering the material remains of the past. As such, it constitutes a body of skills providing data that can be used by various disciplines. In addition to prehistoric archeology, there is Near Eastern, classical, medieval, colonial, and even industrial archeology.

Methods of Prehistory

History and prehistory thus complement one another and round out the chronicle of man's development. They differ, however, in the kinds of evidence they use and the kind of reconstructions they attempt. The historian has as raw data accounts of the ideas or behavior of human beings; the prehistorian, on the other hand, must be content to study the limited material remains of past cultures that have been able to resist decomposition and are recovered by the archeologist. For the oldest periods, only archeological and physical anthropological evidence is available and the prehistorian concentrates on working out typologies of stone tools and correlating them with geological and paleontological sequences. For more recent times, ethnological and linguistic evidence, as well as legends and historical accounts, can often be used to supplement the archeological data. If, as most anthropologists do, we define culture as the ideas or symbols that man acquires as a member of society, then the prehistorian, for the most part, has no cultural data to work with. On the contrary, he has only *artifacts,* sometimes called "material culture," which are themselves a product of culture, and it is from these very limited and largely technological kinds of evidence that his picture of the past must be inferred.

Prehistoric studies are thus by their very nature anonymous. Most of their energies are devoted to *inferring* the outlines of ancient ways of life and tracing their development over time. Because of the nature of the evidence, these inferences are often of a fairly general sort. In the absence of historical records, for example, Napoleon's invasion of Russia could be inferred only from the distribution of burnt villages, laboriously recovered by archeological excavation and dated by various methods to approximately the same time. The discovery of weapons and equipment of western European origin might indicate that the group (or groups) responsible for their destruction came from the west and it might also be apparent from the archeological record that the native inhabitants soon regained control of the region. Even this much interpretation, however, would require a good deal of spadework. Such matters as the identity of the major personalities involved, the delineation of national boundaries, and a detailed understanding of the power politics of the period—not to mention who won what battles—would all be beyond the prehistorian's ability to infer.

Since only artifacts or "material culture" (which as we have seen are not culture at all) survive in the archeological record, the reconstruction of prehistoric cultures and events depends largely on a knowledge of the relationships that exist between material objects and human behavior in living cultures. The basic method of interpreting the archeological evidence, then, must be by analogy with existing cultures or known historical situations. Unfortunately, the study of these relationships is a relatively neglected field and most of the theoretical inadequacies of prehistory are also the limitations of anthropology and of the social sciences as a whole.

The work of the prehistorian, like that of the historians implicitly involves two processes. First, he must attempt to visualize the way of life of a people who existed in far different times and, secondly, he must attempt to explain the processes that are involved in the transition from one period to another. True, archeologists can and have constructed cultural chronologies without attempting to discover the nature of the cultures involved. The latter step, however, is a logical prelude to any meaningful study of culture change, inasmuch as one must comprehend *what* is changing in order to understand *how* it changes (W. W. Taylor 1948).

Models

Prehistory is not an experimental discipline. It does not aim, like physics or chemistry, to establish general regularities, and then demonstrating their truth by repeated experiment. It attempts, instead, to explain what has happened in the past to particular groups of people. Like paleontology, historical geology, or modern history, it seeks to explain events rather than to generalize from them (Nagel 1961:547–551). Explanations are ideally made in the light of the most complete evidence and the best theoretical frameworks currently available (Lowther 1962). The accuracy of such explanations can only be tested by their ability to withstand the accumulation of new evidence and the development of more sophisticated theories about the nature of culture. The excavation of new sites may completely alter interpretations based on more limited data, but interpretations may also be revised because of theoretical advances in related fields such as linguistics or cultural anthropology. Prehistorians tend to regard any interpretation as an approximation of reality that is subject to revision or even complete reinterpretation at any time. It is no more possible to write a final account of Predynastic Egypt than it is to write a final history of the reign of Elizabeth I.

Recently, British prehistorians have begun to refer to the various conceptual frameworks they use to interpret archeological data as *models* (Piggott 1961:11, 12;

1965:5–8). Models come in many varieties and vary in importance according to their explanatory power. Some reflect ideas about the functional relationship between different aspects of culture; others ideas about different sorts of historical processes. The most popular models are technological and materialistic ones, largely as Piggott has observed (1965:7) "because [the archeologist's point of view] is based on the products of ancient technology." Archeologists who attempt to interpret their material from a technological point of view are in effect trying to view a whole culture in relationship to the technology. Other functional models attempt to view entire cultures from an economic, social, or even ideological perspective. Historical models view cultural development as cyclical or evolutionary, unilineal or multilineal. They may also reflect the prehistorian's opinion as to whether diffusion or parallel invention is a more important historical process. Finally, there are models that embody the prehistorian's view of the relationship between different categories of historical data. These models concern problems such as whether or not continuities in material culture necessarily indicate ethnic and linguistic continuities in a particular region (Palmer 1965:180–181).

The term is thus applicable to any well-defined concept that prehistorians use to interpret their data. Very often, several models are used in combination. The model is important because it helps the archeologist to make explicit (at least in his own mind) the assumptions about the nature of culture that underlie his interpretation of the evidence. Because of the often incomplete and limited nature of the evidence which the prehistorian has at his disposal, theories about the nature of culture play a considerably more prominent role in determining his interpretation of the data than they do a historian's. It is regrettable, but true, that in studies of human behavior the less data one has to work with, the more important becomes the role that must be played by inadequate and often erroneous conceptions of the nature of human behavior.

Conclusion

In the following chapters we will examine various concepts and techniques that prehistorians use to study the prehistory of a particular area. A general discussion of concepts in Chapters 2 to 5 is followed, in Chapter 6, by a critical examination of the way in which these concepts have been used to interpret the development of culture in Predynastic Egypt. No attempt is made to discuss archeological techniques as such. Chapters 2 and 3 will investigate the kinds of problems prehistorians deal with and the necessity of distinguishing among race, language and culture, on the one hand, and between society and culture, on the other. Chapter 4 will examine the concepts used to describe culture change, particularly those associated with migration, diffusion and independent development. Finally, in Chapter 5 we will discuss the concepts of social development that describe the networks of social relations within which cultural development takes place. In this way we hope to provide a set of concepts that can be used to explain the historical development of a people in the absence of written records and to provide some idea of the limitations of these concepts and the circumstances under which they may be used.

For empirical reasons, prehistorians tend to define some terms differently from the way ethnologists define them; likewise, not all prehistorians use the same terms in the same way. When these differences are important, the reasons for them will be explained; and not a single definition will be given without going into alternative usages. In most cases, these variations will cause little difficulty for the student.

Essentially, the study of prehistory requires the imaginative application of ethnological findings to archeological data. It is hoped that this study may help to provide a clearer appreciation of the fact that prehistory and ethnology are not independent disciplines, but related parts of the single discipline of anthropology. Although the data available for the study of the past and present are quite different, ethnologists and prehistorians are both concerned with human behavior and the interpretations they offer are influenced by their understanding of the universal properties of this behavior.

2

Race, Language, and Culture

The Independence of the Variables

ANTHROPOLOGISTS traditionally have been interested in the study of primitive "tribes" or "peoples." Although the term tribe is defined in a variety of ways, it is frequently described as a group possessing a territory of its own, and whose "members feel that they share certain distinctive features of culture and language" (Goldschmidt 1959:151). The members of a tribe also are frequently alleged to conform to a particular physical type. Generally, it has been assumed that the tribes described in the anthropological literature are objective divisions of humanity rather than units arbitrarily created by the people who have studied them.

The anthropological belief that tribes constitute cohesive social units, stemmed in part from a belief that most primitive people regard outsiders with fear and suspicion, and tend to avoid them. The idea that each tribe had its own well-defined physical and cultural characteristics was based on the theory that people who interact freely with one another will tend to retain and develop traits in common, whereas those who are separated from each other will tend to develop along their own lines. The tendency to attribute all change to the differentiation of originally similar tribal units led prehistorians to believe that racial, cultural, and linguistic[1] differences all originated as a result of the same ethnic separations. As groups spread they tended to develop regional variations which, in turn, gave rise to new cultures. Pursuing this concept, it became logical to assume that tribes that presently are similar in culture or physical type, are so because their bearers shared a common origin.

This particular view of culture history, was based, however, on a serious

---

[1] By treating language separately from the rest of culture I do not mean to imply that language is not a part of culture. As a self-contained system, however, it is susceptible to independent analysis and its history is often different from that of other aspects of culture.

fallacy; namely, that the racial, cultural, and linguistic differences among various peoples are all the result of the same process of differentiation (Sapir 1921:121–235). It quickly led to the conclusion that any sort of similarity between two groups was evidence of a genetic relationship between them and that, therefore, the history of any group could be reconstructed from a patchwork of different types of data. For example, if several unrelated cultures were associated with racially similar types, it was believed that it could be assumed that these people had once constituted a single ethnic group and that cultural differentiation merely had gone on faster than racial differentiation. Hence, Africanists began to talk about cultures of "Negro" or "Hamitic" (Caucasoid) origin, as if at one time there had been a one-to-one correlation between race and culture in that area (MacGaffey 1966). Likewise, if a number of different tribes spoke related languages, it was assumed that they had once been a single people with a common culture, and that any differences between them now were the result of changes that had taken place since the original group had broken up. Any linguistic, cultural, or racial similarities between peoples were interpreted as evidence that the groups involved had constituted a single ethnic group at some time in the past and differences between them were seen as the result of subsequent modifications. Thus, whenever data of one sort were insufficient to establish an historical relationship between two groups, data of other sorts could always be relied on.

From the start, however, grave problems confronted this method of interpretation and, had there not been so little data of any sort to go on, it probably would have been abandoned sooner than it was. In particular, it seemed impossible to establish any sort of hierarchy for the relative rate of change in race, language, and culture. The genetic constitution of American Negroes may, in part, be of African origin, but their language and culture are of European origin. In like manner, American culture has shown surprising continuity in spite of the absorption of millions of immigrants who are not of the same Anglo-Saxon stock as the original settlers. The ability of human beings to learn new languages and new modes of behavior, as well as the capacity of social systems to assimilate newcomers, has meant that time and time again the racial, linguistic, and cultural history of groups has followed different paths and, consequently, such similarities between groups are no proof that either the people or their culture shared a common origin. Because of cultural diffusion, people who are descended from a common ancestor may no longer share the same, or even a similar, culture; likewise, because of genetic drift, people who possess historically related cultures need share little genetic material in common. It is fairly obvious that gene flow and the diffusion of language and culture are not exceptions to the normal course of human development, but are at least as characteristic of it as is the development of differences through gradual separation.

Edward Sapir (1921) and Franz Boas (1940) summarized these objections when they pointed out that race, language, and culture had to be studied separately and their history treated as independent variables. Their experience with culture areas in North America had shown that traits tended to spread out from their point of origin and that as a result of this prolonged diffusion similar cultures are sometimes shared by people with very different physical and linguistic characteristics. Hence, the latter characteristics cannot be used to provide clues for the reconstruction of culture history, any more than cultural criteria can be used to reconstruct the history of the languages or physical type associated with any particular group. Examples to illustrate this can be drawn from European history. The Romance languages are all evolved forms of Latin, but only a small number of Romance speakers can possibly be the biological decendants of the citizens of ancient Rome. Similarly, the fact that the majority of European nations speak related languages does not explain why they possess a similar culture. Much of the culture of modern Europe is not the heritage from a remote past, but rather is the product of experiences shared through diffusion long after the various languages and nations of modern Europe had come into being. Europeans who speak non-Indo-European languages, such as Basque, Finnish, and Hungarian, have participated in this development no less than have other Europeans.

Because a good deal is known about the history of Europe during the past 2000 years no one would maintain that the most important cultural similarities in this area are vestiges of a common Indo-European culture many thousands of years old. Indeed, the great similarities in European culture, compared with the linguistic variation and the failure of linguistic and cultural (let alone political) boundaries to coincide, would immediately cast doubt on such an hypothesis, even if no historical data were available. Very often such obvious incongruities between racial, linguistic, and cultural distributions prevent prehistorians from confusing these three sorts of data. Sometimes, however, fortuitous correspondences cloud the issue. For many years, the similar distribution of the Iroquoian languages and "Iroquoian" culture in the region of the lower Great Lakes was interpreted as proof that this culture had developed prior to the separation of the Iroquoian peoples into the various tribes that existed in early historic times (Parker 1916). The minor cultural differences among the various tribes were interpreted as recent products of fragmentation. The Iroquoian-looking culture of certain Algonkian-speaking tribes, such as the Mahican and Delaware, was interpreted as the result of "acculturation" to Iroquoian ways, while "Algonkian" traits found among the Iroquoians were attributed to trait diffusion in the opposite direction. The Iroquoians were generally regarded as late arrivals in the Northeast, who had come there as a single group with a common language and culture.

Today, an improved knowledge of Iroquoian archeology and linguistics makes it clear that the various tribal dialects had differentiated long before the development of the culture that characterized the Iroquoian peoples in historic times (Lounsbury 1961). Moreover, Iroquoian culture appears to have developed out of the earlier cultures of the Northeast, hitherto believed to have been associated exclusively with Algonkian-speaking peoples (MacNeish 1952). The similar cultures of the various tribes appear to have been the result, not of the differentiation of a single culture, but rather of shared development in late prehistoric times. For reasons such as this, prehistorians have realized that they must treat the history of race, language, and culture as separate problems.

Evidence that can be used to study the past is basically of two different sorts. The first is that recovered by archeology; the second is that of contemporary situations that can be used as a basis for making inferences about conditions and events in the past.

Cultural History

In the study of culture history, the most important evidence is that provided by archeology (McCall 1964:28–37). This evidence consists of both the products of human manufacture, and the context in which the products are found. From this material the prehistorian can reconstruct the economy, the social and political organization, and the art and beliefs of ancient cultures. He can also use it to study the development and spread of different types of artifacts and to trace the relationship between different cultures. The great advantage of archeological evidence, especially since the development of carbon 14 and other geochronometric methods of dating, is the control one has over the chronology. It is possible to pinpoint both cultures and individual objects in time, as well as place, and to evaluate more precisely the historical relationships among them.

The main weakness of archeological evidence is the limited range of materials that survives. As we have noted, social relationships and real culture (in the sense of ideas) must be inferred from material culture. While it is usually somewhat easy to deduce subsistence patterns from material artifacts, it is considerably more difficult to reconstruct social organization and ideology (C. Hawkes 1954:161–162). Even subsistence patterns are not always self-evident, since artifacts vary in their ability to survive according to age, climate, and what they are made of. In very dry climates or in permafrost almost everything survives; in a tropical forest one is fortunate if even stone tools manage to do so.

Anthropologists have also attempted to use the distribution of ethnographic traits as a basis for reconstructing cultural relationships in prehistoric times. Indeed, the term "culture history" is often reserved for this sort of study. While some scholars have limited themselves to reconstructing the history of individual items or segments of culture such as panpipes, outrigger canoes, dice games, or megaliths, others have attempted to work out the history of whole cultures. Both of these efforts involve assumptions about the nature of culture which very frequently are based on elaborate, but arbitrary, schemes of cultural development. Many of the assumptions concern the probability of similar traits having developed independently in different parts of the world, or of their being historically related. Another disadvantage of distributional studies, compared with archeological ones, is the difficulty of determining at what period traits diffused from one area to another or often even of finding out in what direction they moved. Their advantage lies in the fact that they allow anthropologists to study all aspects of culture, not merely those that are reflected in the archeological record. Murdock (1959a:42) argues that the historical reliability of conclusions based on this sort of approach is enhanced if the prehistorian attempts to reconstruct the history of several major categories of traits independently of one another and then cross-checks to see if the various reconstructions support or contradict each other. On the whole, culture historical studies seem to be most reliable when they are used in conjunction with archeological evidence.

Another source of information about the past is the stories living peoples tell about their own history. This is often referred to as the oral tradition (Vansina 1965:1–18; McCall 1964:37–61). It is well known, however, that such traditions frequently reflect contemporary social and political conditions as much as they do historical reality, and that, even in cultures where there is a strong desire to preserve their integrity, such stories may unconsciously be reworked from generation to generation. Even the oral traditions of Polynesia, which were once famous for the fidelity with which they were supposed to be transmitted, are now known to be out of line with archeological and other sorts of evidence (Suggs 1960:47–56). It is no wonder then that many anthropologists doubt the historical reliability of all oral traditions, and that Murdock (1959a:43) has claimed (although he has never documented) that African oral traditions concerning the origins of a tribe are correct less than 25 percent of the time (when they are over a century old). The unreliability of oral traditions is not restricted only to primitive peoples. This could be brought out in a stuly of how middle class American families rework their oral family histories in the light of rising family fortunes.

The scientific study of oral traditions is obviously an exacting task and requires a careful evaluation of the reliability of sources, a study of the stereotyped motifs that may distort historical evidence, the checking of the stories told by one group against comparable information supplied by others and, finally, checking these stories against independent sources of information such as archeological evidence. Used in this way, oral traditions may supply valuable information about the not too distant past. Used uncritically, however, they can be a source of much confusion and misunderstanding in prehistoric studies.

Physical Anthropology

Studies of racial history are also of two types (McCall 1964:101–106). Skeletons belonging to different cultures can be unearthed and through them changes in physical type can be worked out. Where there is enough data, the physical characteristics of various populations can be reconstructed and gradual changes that result from natural selection or the slow diffusion of genes can be distinguished from those resulting from the influx of a new population. When data are available over a wide area, it may also be possible to determine where new traits or new populations came from. The main shortcoming of this approach, like that of cultural archeology, is that, except under very special conditions, relatively few characteristics are preserved. Nonskeletal features, which are the ones most frequently used to distinguish living races, have long since disappeared.

Present racial distributions, on the other hand, provide only limited clues concerning racial history. One can assume, for example, that any pre-Columbian group in the New World is likely to have been of Mongoloid stock, since none other is known among the peoples indigenous to this area. On the other hand, any historical reconstruction based on the assumption that African and Oceanic Negroes are descended from a common ancestor runs up against the possibility of parallel development in similar environments. Only a detailed study of prehistoric skeletons throughout the tropical regions of the Old World can ultimately prove which of these theories is correct.

The reconstruction of more precise historical events from physical types alone is also difficult. The Tutsi of Rwanda, in the African Congo region, have a Nilotic physical type, unlike that of the Hutu whom they rule. Both groups, however, now speak Bantu. Although the differences in physical type between the present-day Tutsi and Hutu are sufficient to show that the former are intruders in this region, and to relate them with the Nilotes to the east, it would be impossible to determine, from this evidence alone, when or along what route the Tutsi migrated into this area. Only archeological evidence, aided perhaps by their own traditions, can provide this information.

Even more dangerous is the basing of theories of population movement on the comparison of ancient skeletal evidence with the physical characteristics of various living peoples. It is foolish to argue, for example, that a group of people living in the Nile Valley around 2000 B.C. is related to the modern Shilluk, since this argument assumes that the gene pool of the latter has remained the same over a 4000-year period. In view of the considerable amount of gene flow that has gone on in Africa during this period, this is something that would have to be proved rather than assumed (Trigger 1965:88). Archeological evidence concerning physical types would be required.

Linguistics

Strictly defined, prehistory is a text-free discipline. Since the prehistorian lacks written evidence about ancient languages, all of his speculations concerning prehistoric times must be based on information derived from present-day languages or at least on linguistic data recorded later than the period he is studying (McCall 1964:62–71). Fortunately, the historical linguist has at his command techniques for working out historical relationships among languages which are much more exact than the comparable procedures available to the culture historian. Whenever several related languages are known, the phonemics, lexicon, and grammar of the ancestral language can be reconstructed with some degree of accuracy. Through the systematic comparison of fundamental vocabulary, genetic relationships between whole languages can be distinguished from superficial borrowings (Greenberg 1957:39) and through lexicostatistical procedures the relative degree of historical relationship between different languages can be worked out with considerable accuracy. The special form of lexicostatistics known as glottochronology shows promise of being able to determine absolute dates for the separation of different languages at least for a period of several thousand years (Gudschinsky 1956).

Working out the geographical distribution of languages in prehistoric times is much more difficult. A linguist may be able to reconstruct a protolanguage, even be able to say when this language was spoken, yet have difficulty in determining where it was spoken or by what culture or group of cultures. In order to handle this situation, linguists, mainly through the application of various culture distribution theories, have worked out certain rules to help determine where a particular language family originated. Such points of origin are sought either near the center of the distribution of the language family's major branches or else where one finds the greatest variation among languages currently belonging to the family (Sapir

1916:76–78). Since, for example, three branches of Nubian are presently found in Kordofan and Darfur, and only one in the Nile Valley, it is likely that the former regions were the original homeland of the Nubian people. This particular conclusion is supported by additional archeological and historical evidence (Trigger 1966a). There are exceptions to these rules, however, and because of historical events—such as the rapid expansion of certain languages in recent times—not all languages are amenable to this sort of analysis.

Attempts to figure out where certain language groups originated have been made by reconstructing the environment that is suggested by cognate words[2] for plants and animals that have survived in the vocabularies of the modern languages belonging to the group. On this basis it has been suggested that Indo-European was originally spoken in a region where salmon were found and where there were beech trees, probably, it is suggested, in the vicinity of the rivers Vestula, Oder, and Elbe (Thieme 1964:594–597).[3] Similar work is presently under way on proto-Bantu (McCall 1964:69). Efforts have been made to use the same technique to reconstruct the culture associated with proto-Indo-European, and in the future, this may allow a closer correlation to be drawn between archeological and linguistic evidence. The principal danger confronting studies of this sort is the possibility that technical terms can diffuse far and wide and thereby give the false impression of being part of the protolanguage.

Recently, especially in the study of African prehistory, there has been a tendency to place too much trust in language distributions as conclusive evidence of ethnic movements (Lewis 1966:38; MacGaffey 1966:13–17). It must be remembered that languages can spread without major population movements, as Latin spread among the subject peoples of the western Roman Empire and that people, when moving, do not always carry their ancestral language with them. Caution is needed not to interpret the diffusion of languages as a phenomenon resulting only from the migration of peoples.

Conclusion

Following these lines of investigation, it is possible to learn something about the racial, linguistic, and cultural changes that took place in prehistoric times. Each of these fields must be investigated independently, using the data that are appropriate to it. Only when this has been done, is it possible to investigate the relationships that have existed among these different categories of data in specific historical situations.

---

[2] Cognate words are words appearing in two or more languages that can be shown to be derived from a common ancestral word.

[3] This particular conclusion does not seem to be supported, however, by archeological evidence. (See Gimbutas 1963.)

3

Society and Culture

Definitions

SOCIETY can be defined as the network of habitual social relations formed by people interacting with one another; culture can be characterized briefly as the ideas that men carry around in their heads. While social interaction can be observed, culture can only be inferred from what men say and do (Radcliffe-Brown 1957:43–75, 92–104; Wallace 1961:6–44). Material culture, which is the product of a very limited range of human behavior, constitutes, therefore, a limited basis for the reconstruction of the past.

Inasmuch as all social interaction is based upon ideas and expectations which act as a guide to behavior, there is a close relationship between society and culture. Moreover, people who are part of the same social system can be expected to share many of the same ideas, and because of this, many anthropologists do not differentiate sharply between society and culture, preferring simply to lump them together as sociocultural phenomena. Almost inevitably, however, prehistorians are predisposed to think in terms of culture rather than social structure. This is a natural result of their use of artifacts as data and the fact that much of their work consists of making rather low-level inferences about the roles that these artifacts played in the culture of which they were a part. Although prehistorians have always been interested in reconstructing prehistoric ways of life in their totality, they usually have treated the social organization, as well as the beliefs and values, of prehistoric peoples as disjointed traits rather than as systems that should be analyzed on their own terms. While they have been concerned to know, for example, whether a particular culture was matrilineal or patrilineal, the answer was regarded as another trait to be enumerated along with tanged arrowheads and ground stone axes as attributes of that culture. Very few efforts have been made to analyse prehistoric social organizations from a structural point of view. It is only recently, as some prehistorians have tried to study prehistoric social organization, that they have become aware of the limitations involved in treating social systems as aspects of culture, rather than as systems susceptible to analysis in their own right (Deetz 1965; Longacre 1964). The problems involved in correlating these two approaches are gradually prompting a restudy of the relationship between society and culture and the significance of this relationship for prehistoric studies.

Cultural Units

Prehistorians have tried to delineate cultural configurations, or patterns, in the assemblages of artifacts they uncover. To aid in this, they have devised various systems of ordered units to compare these assemblages. The primary unit of comparison is the *component,* which is defined as a single period of occupation in the history of a given site (Willey and Phillips 1958:21–22). For a component to be meaningful, the time segment that is isolated must be short enough so that one can assume that no significant cultural change took place during it, and that all of the material associated with the component is therefore representative of the people who inhabited the site at a given point in the development of their culture. The various components that are present in a site that has been occupied for a long period of time can usually be distinguished from each other by means of natural or artificial stratigraphy.

Because so many components are found, they are invariably grouped together to form larger and historically more meaningful units. When prehistory was in its infancy, these units were extremely general ones, intended merely to reflect certain general *stages* in a pattern of development that was assumed to be unilineal and universal. An early example of a classification of this sort is Christian Thomsen's division of prehistory into three ages of stone, bronze and iron. In the second half of the nineteenth century, when archeologists became aware of the great antiquity of man and when the relationship between prehistoric archeology and Pleistocene geology was very close, efforts to construct universal schemes of cultural development became increasingly popular. Gabriel de Mortillet's subdivision of the Paleolithic Age into the Acheulian, Mousterian, Solutrean, and Magdalenian periods, each of which was characterized by a particular lithic industry, was in many ways an attempt to continue the geological sequence down to modern times, using cultural instead of paleontological criteria to define each epoch.[1]

It was soon apparent, however, that such analogies between paleontology and prehistory were far from satisfactory. For one thing, different parts of the world had been, and were, at different stages of development at the same time, so that the correspondence between "stage" and "age" was not as close in culture history as it appeared to be in the more slowly moving realm of geology. Then too, it was obvious that, partly for environmental and partly for historical reasons, the cultural content of various societies that were considered to be at the same stage of development was often radically different. By the middle of the nineteenth century,

---

[1] This concept influenced anthropological theory for a long time. In 1889, in a famous study of the development of laws of marriage and descent, Tylor likened human institutions to geological strata and continued: "They succeed each other in series substantially uniform over the globe . . . but shaped by similar human nature."

Daniel Wilson had noted that the artifacts associated with the Danes and Anglo-Saxons were dissimilar, although both groups lived side by side and were at a similar stage of cultural development (Trigger 1966*b*:8). Finally, as time passed, it became increasingly clear that all cultures in the world had not passed through the same sequence of development.

Thus, while the concept of stages was never completely abandoned, prehistorians sought to interpret the archeological record in greater detail by constructing smaller and less universalistic groupings of components. These units are generally called *cultures* or *phases,* the latter term being most commonly used in American, the former in Old World archeology. Although defined almost entirely in terms of characteristic artifact assemblages, and very often in terms of a few types of distinctive artifacts (Kluckhohn 1962:75–76; Rouse 1965:5), archeological cultures have generally been regarded as products of people sharing a common way of life, that is, as cultures in the same sense that ethnologists define them. Such ethnological cultures are ongoing traditions, of which material remains are presumed to represent various stages in their development. Or as Lewis Mumford has vividly phrased it:

> Only material culture ever remains stratified. The nonmaterial culture is fibrous in nature; though the long threads may be broken, they go through every stratum and, even when they are out of sight, they are continuously present. (Kraeling and Adams 1960:227).

The most serious question involved in such an assumption is whether identity or close similarity in material remains indicates identity in all aspects of culture, including language, social structure, and ideology.

Some prehistorians have tried to equate archeological cultures with particular "tribes" or "peoples." In 1911, the German archeologist, Gustav Kossinna, postulated the following relationships:

> Sharply defined archaeological culture-provinces coincide at all times with quite definite peoples or tribes; cultural regions are ethnic regions, culture groups are peoples (Childe 1956:28).

In 1956, V. Gordon Childe formulated a definition of culture as follows:

> [A culture is] an assemblage of artifacts that recur repeatedly associated together . . . the arbitrary peculiarities of the . . . objects are assumed to be the concrete expressions of the common social traditions that bind together a people (Childe 1956:2).

Both of these definitions stress the sociological dimensions of an archeological culture by viewing it as the product of close social interaction and by identifying basic cultural units with particular tribes or peoples.

Other prehistorians, having felt that definitions of this sort require unwarranted assumptions about the nature of culture, prefer more objective ones based on the amount of formal similarity among the artifacts found in the components being compared. Willey and Phillips (1958:22), for example, have adopted the following definition of a culture:

an archaeological unit possessing traits sufficiently characteristic to distinguish it from all other units similarly conceived, whether of the same or other cultures or civilizations, spatially limited to the order of magnitude of a locality or region and chronologically limited to a relatively brief interval of time.

This definition is obviously one based on similarities and differences in content and in spite of its present ambiguities, could conceivably be operationalized in a quantitative fashion. Moreover, it deliberately leaves open the question of what sort or sorts of social grouping can be associated with an archeological culture. Willey and Phillips (1958:48–49) express the opinion that no one type of social unit corresponds to an archeological culture and, moreover, that the boundaries of social and cultural units are rarely coextensive.

Serious problems are raised by both sorts of definitions. Let us examine, (1) Why the social aspect must be taken account of in a definition of culture? (2) What are the dangers of doing so? and (3) How this seeming contradiction can be resolved.

It is obvious that internal variations can and do characterize certain cultures. The urban nucleus of a small city state differs from a farming village outside its gates, just as a temporary Iroquois fishing camp does not resemble one of their main villages. The tools, as well as the houses, found in an Eskimo winter camp near the sea may be different from those found in summer camps located far inland (W. E. Taylor 1966). All of these differences, however, are primarily ecological or social. If the archeological concept of a culture is to meet the ethnological requirement of representing the total design for living of a people who share a common historical tradition, then the definition must be flexible enough to embrace the variations in the style of life found within such a pattern. This eliminates the possibility of all archeological cultures being defined in terms of only the formal similarities among their components.

In complex societies, life styles are likely to be strongly differentiated along class lines. Sometimes, whole communities are inhabited by members of one class, so that there is a correlation, in archeological terms, between components and social classes. Because of the cultural differences between sites inhabited by the elite on the one hand, and the lower classes on the other, these sites are sometimes regarded as belonging to different cultures. It has been suggested, for example, that the Mayan peasantry and elite might conceivably be treated as two separate peoples or ethnic groups (Rouse 1965:9–10). It is unlikely, however, that these two classes or social groups thought of themselves as ethnically distinct in the same way, for example, that Belgians and Germans do. Both shared a common history and were interdependent parts of a single social and economic system. The ethnologist's idea of a culture is of a total design for living; by this criterion, the Mayan peasantry and elite can at most be considered as subcultures of a common Mayan culture.

Another problem is that of defining external boundaries. Anthropologists formerly conceived of cultures as being internally homogeneous (allowing for class differences) and possessing well-defined boundaries. Today they are increasingly aware that cultural variations often occur along clines or gradients as well as at sharply defined boundaries (Leach 1960, 1961b:3). Moreover, the boundaries of cultures tend to vary according to the nature and the degree of specificity of the criteria that are chosen to define them. Under these conditions, the definition of cultural units often tends to be highly arbitrary, and for the archeologist working with limited evidence, the problem is even greater. On the basis of a superficial survey, he may define an archeological culture, which on closer investigation turns out to be a whole series of related cultures (that is, what the ethnologist would call a culture area). On the other hand, there are situations where there is more or less constant variation over a large area, and here culture units must be defined in an essentially arbitrary manner. The conceptual problems that the prehistorian must cope with in defining cultures are very similar to those faced by the physical anthropologist trying to delineate racial groups (Garn 1962:12–22).

It is clear for these reasons alone that no purely formal grouping of sites containing similar assemblages of artifacts will necessarily produce archeological units that are equivalent to the ethnologist's idea of a culture. Implicitly or explicitly, some consideration must be given to social factors.

Social Organization

Many archeologists, as we have already mentioned, treat society as an attribute of culture. To describe a culture, they assemble an inventory of traits which embraces the types of artifacts they have recovered, and make conjectures concerning the nature of the subsistence pattern, social organization and value system.

In *Piecing Together the Past,* V. Gordon Childe (1956:124–131) presents an outline of such an inventory, which (in brief) is as follows:

A. *Economy*
    1. subsistence (habitat, food, warmth, shelter)
    2. industries (stone, metal, bone, wood, etc.)
    3. transport
    4. trade
    5. war

B. *Sociology*
    1. demography
    2. family
    3. town planning
    4. social structure

C. *Ideology*
    1. scientific
    2. religious
    3. artistic
    4. sportive

Martin, Quimby, and Collier (1947) have organized their summary descriptions of the archeological cultures of North America under the general headings of location, human physical type, village plans, livelihood, pottery, tools, utensils and weapons, pipes, ornaments, musical instruments, and burials.

All of these efforts are similar in that they treat society as "social culture," rather than as a system of social relations. There is, of course, no reason not to do this. The Amratian culture of Predynastic Egypt can legitimately be described as characterized by village life and probably lacking any form of state government. It should be understood, however, that this is different from an attempt to reconstruct the social relations of an Amratian village or tribal unit. In the first case, society is being examined as an aspect of culture; in the second, culture is being viewed within the framework of a social system.

Some archeologists, particularly those who have had only a superficial acquaintance with ethnographic data, have held that it is easy to find correlations between cultural configurations and social systems. Many have suggested, for example, that an archeological component corresponds to a community, a culture to a tribe, and a series of related cultures to a culture area (MacWhite 1956:6–9). A brief reflection will show the inadequacy of these conclusions, on every level. Certainly no one would wish to classify a remote fishing camp, used for only a few weeks in the year, or a kill site, where game is butchered, as a community. Among many groups of hunters, a large band will come together at one season of the year and break up into smaller groupings at another. If we equate the term community with the band (in the sense of the maximal group living in face to face association for at least part of the year), then all of the sites occupied by the band in the course of a year must be considered as manifestations of a single community.

It is apparent too, that no single social or political unit is invariably coterminous with a single pattern of material culture. Many examples can be found of people sharing similar material cultures yet having different social, political, or linguistic affiliations. Contrary situations can also be found where members of the same social grouping or tribe follow different ways of life. An example of this are the Fulani, some of whom are nomadic pastoralists, others sedentary cultivators, and all of whom live for the most part as an ethnic minority dispersed among other groups (Murdock 1959a:413–420). In early Dynastic Egypt, the local culture *was* coterminous with the Egyptian kingdom; on the other hand, the region embraced by Mesopotamian culture at the same period was divided up into a series of autonomous city states (Frankfort 1956). Even at a simple food producing level, there are frequently no one-to-one correlations between political, social, and material culture units. Among the Five Nations Iroquois, local archeological cultures can be distinguished which correspond to each (or at least to most) of the five historic tribes (MacNeish 1952). These tribes, however, formed a single political confederacy. Among the neighboring Huron, who resembled the Iroquois in many ways, only one archeological culture has been distinguished, although we know that this group constituted a confederacy divided into four tribes (plus another tribe, the Petun, that was independent of the confederacy). In the Sudan, the Nuer and Dinka share a generally similar material culture, but constitute different and mutually hostile tribes.

It is clear, then, that archeological cultures cannot be correlated in any mechanical fashion with societal groupings such as tribes, bands or nations. The reason for this is not simply a technical one—such as insufficient data—but instead, because distributions of material culture do not necessarily conform with social and political configurations. Childe (1956:133) himself recognized this problem and stated that "the sociological counterpart of an archeological culture can only be designated by the non-committal term "people." *People,* however, is not a technical term, and we must question, therefore, if it has any useful meaning in the manner that Childe employs it. In popular usage, the term implies a designated group sharing a meaningful sense of unity and common identity. This identity, however, rests on many different foundations. The Swiss speak four languages, but share a common sense of political identity; the Kurds, on the other hand, have a strong sense of ethnic identity, although they have never constituted a state, and different parts of their homeland are presently administered by Turkey, Iraq, the USSR, and Iran. Many examples can be found of groups who share similar (and in archeological terms, probably identical) cultures, yet do not share a sense of identity because their first loyalties are focused on state institutions of more limited scope. In the modern world, the various Latin American nations are one case in point, the Scots and English another, and Anglo-Canadians and Americans a third. Moreover, a sense of identification will often vary according to the situation. In more complex societies, especially, an individual may have a wide variety of loyalties, varying from narrow loyalties to his clan or community, outward to the state and to mankind in general (Nadel 1951:184–188).

Thus, a uniform material culture does not constitute proof that the people associated with it necessarily had a strong sense of common identity anymore than differences in material culture prove the lack of such a sense of identity. If, however, the term *people* is used only to designate a group that shared a common material culture (as Childe evidently proposes to use it) then it is redundant and meaningless. Willey and Phillips are correct when they argue that an archeological culture cannot automatically be correlated with any specific societal unit and that social units must be defined in their own terms. Childe and Kossinna are also right when they argue that any definition of an archeological culture that is entirely typological and does not take sociological factors into account runs into the danger of classifying different aspects of the life of the same group as different cultures. To resolve this dilemma, we must reconsider some of the basic concepts of prehistory.

The Concept of the Community

While a culture, in the ethnological sense, is a way of life, it is also an assemblage of traits, each one of which may also be present in neighboring cultures. For this reason, the borders of ethnological cultures are usually defined, at least in part, using societal criteria. Hence, when we speak of the culture of the Nuer, we refer to those traits possessed by a group of people claiming a particular name, whether or not those traits are possessed, individually or almost *in toto,* by neighboring groups. In fact, there are probably few traits that are exclusively Nuer, except for those related to the tribe's assertion of ethnic identity. This kind of association of cultures with particular groups of people is possible only because the ethnologist is able to examine all kinds of traits, including those of ethnic identity. It is difficult for the archeologist to delineate ethnically meaningful boundaries as long as the only data at his disposal concern material culture. Archeological cultures are, and no doubt will remain, units defined primarily in terms of material culture. It must be remembered, therefore, that groupings of components based on these criteria need not correspond to others which attempt to delineate various patterns of social relations. All interpretations begin with components, and it is in the primary analysis of components that alternative strategies can be employed to draw social and cultural units closer together.

A substantial number of inferences can be made concerning the social structure associated with a component. From the archeological data, for example, it can be determined whether the component was a permanent settlement, a seasonal camp, or a special purpose site, such as a butchering place or a flint mine. This sort of information constitutes the basis for making inferences about the community structure associated with components or groups of components. By a community we mean, of course, those groups of people who normally (that is, for at least part of the year) lived in face to face association (Murdock 1949:79). In the case of permanent villages, the main component is usually equivalent to a community, while nearby encampments of the same culture often turn out to be part-time settlements associated with the main village. Among hunting and gathering cultures, however, it may be possible only to define communities statistically rather than to delineate them in terms of actual settlement patterns. The archeologist may note, for example, that in a particular region he finds only one large winter settlement for every ten smaller summer ones. This might suggest that a band having lived together during the winter separated to form smaller and more scattered units during the summer. Where sites are distributed fairly evenly, it might not be possible to determine exactly which summer camps were inhabited by the people who lived in a particular winter encampment. Nevertheless, it would be possible to say something about the average size and composition of the groups that had inhabited the region. In theory, the effort to define communities among primitive societies should reduce to a minimum the danger that the archeologist would attribute seasonal expressions of the same culture to different groups. In practise, however, it is frequently difficult to determine the exact contemporaneity of sites and the period of the year when each site was inhabited. This means that our control of the data is often far from perfect and that interpretations usually involve a number of unproved assumptions. Nevertheless, once the archeologist has defined a set of community patterns, he can proceed to assign those communities possessing similar material remains to the same archeological culture.

Among more complex societies, certain complications arise. In them, we find communities that are different from one another, yet are linked together in a network of functional interdependence. In a few such societies the ruling elite are of different origins from the people they rule and, in situations where both groups tend to preserve their own traditions, we may be justified in speaking of these groups as ethnically distinct (Murdock 1959a:350). Where the rulers and peasantry share the same cultural background and are distinguished from each other only by their standard of living and degree of cultural refinement, these differences in life style are usually considered as being of a subcultural order. Hence, even if whole communities are part of one or the other of these subcultures, they are still part of a single culture.

An archeological culture can thus be defined as a group of communities sharing a similar material culture or displaying no greater variation in material culture than can be explained on the basis of occupational or class differences within a single cultural tradition. A culture is thus defined in terms of the typological similarities found among socially defined minimal units (that is, communities). While there is no agreement as to the exact degree of similarity involved, there is, however, the further stipulation that a culture should normally reflect a total design for living.

What is of greater importance, however, is that communities can also be used to trace relationships other than those based on similarity in material culture. We have already noted that the political organization of the early city states of Mesopotamia was different than the one found in Egypt. Even without written records, the excavation of many walled cities of similar size would suggest the possibility of city state organization in Mesopotamia; whereas the royal funerary centers in Egypt, of which there is one for each reign, would suggest that the country was under some kind of powerful central control. The boundaries of many known kingdoms do not conform with the boundaries of the cultures that are associated with them. Indeed, many of the great empires of the past have embraced a large number of distinct cultures. In order to make inferences concerning prehistoric political units it is necessary to map settlements over large areas and, even then, the results are not always satisfactory. At the time of the Spanish conquest, highland Mexico was divided into many small city states, each with a capital city containing the main temples and palaces. A recent survey of the Teotihuacan Valley, near Mexico City, has attempted, with some success, to work out the pattern of city states in earlier times (Sanders 1965). In the Mayan area, however, there is still debate as to whether the large ceremonial centers were each the capital of an independent state or whether they were regional headquarters within a larger Mayan empire (Coe 1961).

Under rare circumstances, communities can also be grouped according to their linguistic affiliations, although this cannot be done with certainty using archeological data alone. Unfortunately, although certain general distributions of languages in prehistoric times have been worked out, it is often difficult, if not impossible, to draw linguistic boundaries with a high degree of precision. Frequently what is done is to associate a single language with a particular archeological culture. There are, of course, dangers in doing this. It is unlikely, for example, that archeological evidence alone would allow prehistorians of the future to determine which villages in northern Scotland presently speak Gaelic and which speak English. Similarly, while many archeologists have identified the La Tene culture in western Europe with Celtic-speaking peoples, it has become clear, as a result of historical and linguistic research, that not all the Celtic peoples had a La Tene culture, while some people who were not Celts did (De Laet 1957:87). The main problem in all linguistic studies of this kind is the difficulty of controlling geographical factors that we described above. Whenever it is possible to reconstruct linguistic distributions independently of material culture, it is desirable to do so.

Archeologists are also interested in tracing patterns of economic interaction. These studies, however, may be concerned less with individual societies and cultures than with the flow of goods over long distances and the social mechanisms involved in this Among the kinds of site worthy of special attention are the Indus Valley trading establishments that existed outside some Sumerian cities or the Assyrian trading posts that were built on the outskirts of Anatolian towns around the end of the third millennium B.C. (J. Hawkes and Woolley 1963:454; 609–610). Data of these kind not only help to track down sources of raw materials and manufactured goods, and the routes over which they travelled, but also to help solve such problems as whether trade was controlled by independent merchants or by the governments of various states. By adopting a flexible point of view, and using the community as a point of departure, the prehistorian is able to treat the social relationships involved as a meaningful network rather than merely having to view trade as external contacts between different archeological cultures.

Treating the community as a basic unit, it becomes possible to link these units together using various criteria such as artifact types, political organization, economic relations, and language. The overall patterns which emerge when different criteria are applied are far from identical. The flexibility of this approach allows the prehistorian to examine various aspects of the past on their own terms rather than within a rigid framework of arbitrarily defined cultures. In this way, reconstructions approaching the complexity of living cultures may be achieved.

The Historical Significance of Material Culture

A further question of culture-historical significance is whether the various types of artifacts found in a single component, or in a culture, can be treated on an equal basis as being representative of that culture, or whether each type of artifact should be treated as one whose historical significance should be examined independently. Two papers, both published recently, come to mind which illustrate the advantages of the latter approach.

The first is James V. Wright's (1965) study of the historical archeology of the Indian tribes of Northern Ontario in the seventeenth century. These tribes are known to have been for the most part Ojibwa-speakers, who, sharing a common way of life based on hunting and gathering, contrasted sharply with the sedentary agricultural tribes living in the warmer and more fertile regions to the south. Because the Ojibwa bands were deeply involved in the fur trade, they probably moved about more freely in the seventeenth century than they had previously.

Examining the ceramics from five historic sites in this region, Wright found no consistent assemblage of traits that would demonstrate any close geographical or temporal relationship among them. Instead, he found that styles borrowed from regions as far apart as Southern Ontario, Michigan, Wisconsin, and Manitoba occurred in different frequencies in each of the five sites. Apparently, the pottery types possessed by any particular band were a more sensitive indicator of those groups outside the area with whom the band was in contact than they were as indicators of any sort of Ojibwa ethnic identity. Probably, this lack of a strong native pottery tradition is a reflection of the relative unimportance of pottery among the northern hunting peoples; certainly the situation Wright encountered is very different from that found farther south among the Iroquoian-speaking peoples, where local pottery traditions were very strong and variations in shape and decoration constitute sensitive indicators of ethnic divisions. This example, incidentally, is a warning that the same category of evidence (in this case pottery) can have a very different significance in different cultures.

Among the stone tools from his Ojibwa sites, Wright found a much greater degree of spatial and temporal consistency, suggesting that these were a more indigenous aspect of the material culture of the region and hence are better evidence for working out spatial and temporal relationships. But the lithic tool kit represents an important part of the technology by which the people of this region exploited their environment. Hence, widespread similarities in stone tools in this part of the world are probably more an indication of a similar adaptation to a common environment than they are of ethnic identity. For this reason, stone tools are probably no better an indication of ethnic relationships in northern Ontario than are ceramic types. The only basis for attributing all of these sites to a single linguistic group is the ethnohistorical evidence.

The second study is William Y. Adam's (1965) discussion of the X-Group, or Ballana culture in the northern Sudan. This culture flourished between the third and sixth centuries A.D., after the decline of the Meroitic civilization in that region. Archeologists, who for the most part had been excavating cemeteries, had noticed various differences between these two cultures and concluded that the former had developed outside of Lower Nubia and had been introduced there by an invasion of newcomers, who had completely swamped the Meroites and their civilization. The region where the Ballana culture was supposed to have originated was not discovered, but it was variously postulated to be located among the Beja to the east, or the Berbers to the west, or the Nubians to the south. The obvious similarities between the Meroitic and Ballana cultures were attributed either to common traditions underlying both or to Meroitic influences on the Ballana culture prior to its entry into Lower Nubia.

In Adams' study of the Ballana culture he divides the archeological evidence into a number of different classes. He notes that in domestic architecture and settlement patterns the continuity from Meroitic to Ballana times is unbroken; in political organization and religion (as represented in buildings and inscriptions) there is evidence of the breakup of the Meroitic state and the decline of the state religion; in pottery and domestic arts there is the almost total ascendancy of Roman and Byzantine influences, and in burial practices there appears a new orientation for the body and the introduction of retainer burials involving human sacrifice. The evidence thus indicates cultural continuity in some aspects of culture and also changes that took place as a result of diffusion from Egypt. Presumably, with the decline of the main centers of Meroitic culture farther south, Lower Nubia turned to Egypt for future cultural inspiration. In the sphere of material culture, only the new form of burial suggests the possibility of any outside influences of non-Egyptian origin and might be used to support the idea of a migration of people into Nubia at this time. Even with this feature, however, there is a strong possibility of independent invention. Adams' analysis of different kinds of traits clearly shows how unfounded was the assumption that there is one explanation for all of the changes that took place at, or near, the start of the Ballana period, and also how dangerous it can be to rely too heavily on one type of evidence, such as burial practices (or perhaps even pottery).

These papers demonstrate rather well the limitations of attempts to define cultures and interpret historical events merely by comparing the formal similarities and differences among the artifacts recovered from different components. For ecological or cultural reasons, the historical significance of different types of artifacts may vary from culture to culture. Moreover, the historical significance of particular categories of material culture is not necessarily the same in every culture.

This suggests that it is only possible to understand the historical significance of a trait, if we first know something about its functional significance or role in the society of which it was a part (Steward and Setzler 1938). This is in one sense a pessimistic conclusion, since it is frequently difficult to determine the functional significance of traits. In spite of very careful microscopic studies of wear patterns, even the technological function of many paleolithic tools still remains unknown (Semenov 1964) and archeologists have developed scarcely any methods for determining the role of objects that are doubtfully labelled religious or magical (Sears 1961). A fuller understanding of the functional significance of artifacts within their total culture will not only aid historical reconstructions, but will also serve as an example of the close interdependence of the social and cultural approaches in prehistory.

4

Culture Change

AMONG PREHISTORIANS, the study of culture change is primarily an examination of invention, diffusion, and migration (Kroeber 1948:344–571). It is generally believed that these three concepts, judiciously applied, can be used to explain all of the changes observed in the archeological record. A large literature has grown up around each of them and an even larger one around the controversies concerning the relative importance of each as a factor in culture change.

Invention

By the term invention or innovation is meant the creation of any new idea, that is, the conceiving of something not previously known to the inventor. An invention is a "mutation" that comes about through the modification of an idea in the light of experience or the combining of several old ideas to produce a new one (Kroeber 1948:352–374; R. B. Dixon 1928:33–58). The concept definitely excludes the acquisition of new ideas from a source external to the individual. Most innovations, like the majority of biological mutations, are minor ones and are unimportant, either because they remain idiosyncratic or because they replicate something that is already known to others. The solving of a cross-word puzzle is an innovation of the latter sort.

The term invention is, therefore, most often reserved for a socially significant innovation, whether it be a new machine or technical process, an institutional change—such as the development of representative government—or a scientific or philosophical discovery. Innovations may be the result of either planned research or accidental discovery. Many important changes, particularly in the social sphere, do not come about as the result of a single discovery but rather are the cumulative product of many small innovations, often made simultaneously by different people.

Diffusion and Migration

Diffusion is the name given to the process by which an invention gains social acceptance. It refers to the spread of new ideas or new units of culture from one person or group to another. If a parallel can be drawn between innovation and mutation, diffusion may be described as the process of selection by which a trait either is added to those that are already part of a culture or else manages to replace an existing trait. The successful diffusion of a trait is the result of a process of evaluation in which individuals and groups come to appreciate and accept it. This evaluation is made in terms of the needs and belief systems of the culture involved and the choices made by one culture may not be the choices made by another (Erasmus 1961:17–97). Particularly in the area of technology, the acceptance of new traits depends on whether or not they are perceived as promoting a culture's more effective exploitation of its environment.

Some anthropologists distinguish between primary diffusion, which takes place within the culture in which a trait was invented, and secondary diffusion, which is the diffusion of a trait beyond it (R. B. Dixon 1928: 59, 106). It is argued that the chances of a trait diffusing within its culture of invention are greater than the chances of it being accepted by other cultures, where needs and values may be different. Traits may spread independently of one another or in clusters. When an entire foreign culture is accepted by a group, the process is called assimilation (Kroeber 1948:415–428). A cluster of traits which spread together may or may not be functionally interrelated. The former are usually called a "logical trait-complex." One example is the horse-complex, which seems to have evolved in Central Asia, and comprises, in addition to the horse itself, the bridle and bit, saddle, quirt (whip), harness, cart, and the use of mare's milk for food (R. B. Dixon 1928:158). This collection of traits spread throughout much of Northern Asia and, with the exception of the use of mare's milk, throughout Europe. Other clusters of traits may not be functionally related but merely travel together since various contacts exist between groups which permit them to do so. Accidental trait-complexes tend to be more ephemeral than logical ones and are subject to more drastic changes and substitutions.

Diffusion involves the spread of ideas and, as such, must be distinguished from the spread of goods as a result of trade or warfare. The Eskimos, for example, trade with the Europeans for iron goods and these goods have become an important part of their culture. In spite of this, they have never learned to make these tools for themselves. In other words, while the idea of using iron tools has spread to the Eskimos, the ideas of iron production have not. From a cultural point of view, the statement that iron tools have diffused to the Eskimos is incorrect. What we mean is that the Eskimos obtain iron tools from the Europeans. The fact that they do so, means that Eskimo culture is no longer self-sufficient, but has become dependent on European technology. This illustrates another characteristic of diffusion.

As a trait moves from one culture to another, it is rare if all of its attributes move with it. The idea of adding an outrigger to a canoe may diffuse from one culture to another, yet in the second culture the boat will probably be built according to local traditions of carpentry, which may be very different from what they were in the original culture. The basic idea of the chemical composition of gunpowder spread from China to Europe, but because the technology and political structure of Europe were different from those of China, gunpowder was developed differently and came to play a very different role in Europe from what it did in China. An extreme example of limited diffusion is the spread of writing from the Americans to the Cherokee in 1821 (Kroeber 1948:369–370). A half-breed Indian by the name of Sequoya did not learn how to read English, but by observing his American neighbors he grasped the basic idea that it was possible to represent sounds with written symbols. Working on his own, he invented a syllabary of 86 characters (many borrowed from the English alphabet, but in no case used to represent their original sound values), which he then used to write his own language. In this example, only the *idea* of writing, not that of the alphabet, let alone the original sound values of the letters, spread from one culture to another. Such extreme examples are sometimes called stimulus diffusion or stimulus invention (Kroeber 1940; 1948:368–370), meaning that only general principles, rather than all of the details associated with a complex invention are diffused, and that these general principles stimulate what is in most respects a new invention. In one sense, almost all examples of diffusion between cultures are examples of stimulus diffusion, since a trait rarely manages, or is required, to carry all of its technological, let alone, conceptual attributes with it from one group to another. In order for a nation, such as China, to build its own atomic bomb, it is not necessary for its scientists to learn how Americans produce a nut or bolt.

It is also important to note that, while diffusion frequently results in the spread of a trait over vast distances, it does so because an idea is transmitted from one person to another. The expansion of a people who carry their culture with them may likewise result in the geographical spread of a trait, but the spread is not diffusion, since no new individuals or groups share the trait after the movement has taken place. By contrast, the learning of the English language and American patterns of behavior by an immigrant to the United States *is* an example of cultural diffusion, although it is one that in no way involves the geographical spread of a trait or trait complex. Diffusion refers to the spread of traits socially from individual to individual, and ultimately from group to group, rather than to their geographical movement.

Because of this, we must thus distinguish between the spread of ideas and the movement of peoples. The latter is usually called *migration*. Often these two concepts are not clearly separated since, it is argued, the spread of ideas always comes about through people meeting and interacting. Frequently, migration is classified as a subset of diffusion and distinctions are drawn between the diffusion of culture that is accomplished through large-scale movements of people and that which is accomplished without it (MacWhite 1956:17). In fact, the situation is more complex and definitions of this kind merely blur the distinction between the spread of ideas and the movement of people. The spread of a people can, for example, lead to the geographical expansion of a culture, without the spread of elements of this culture to new groups (such as was the case with the Viking settlements in the New World); on the other hand, movements of population can be an important agent of cultural diffusion (as in the Spanish conquest and settlement in Mexico). In still other cases, cultures can diffuse without people moving (such as the spread of Latin culture throughout the western Roman Empire) or people can move without the diffusion of culture taking place (the total assimilation of immigrants). The various combinations that are observed of these suggest that the migration of people and the diffusion of ideas are independent concepts that are better kept conceptually separate when we interpret historical phenomena.

Distinguishing Independent Invention, Diffusion, and Migration

The prehistorian is interested in formulating rules that will allow him to distinguish changes in culture resulting from diffusion, migration, and independent development. The data he uses come either from archeological excavations or from distributional studies. By and large, the prehistorian is not interested in investigating these processes on an interpersonal level, but rather in distinguishing how they are involved in the interaction between cultures or large societal units. On this level independent development normally means that the trait was invented inside the culture being investigated, and diffusion means diffusion between cultures.

Evidence of the act of invention is rare in the archeological record. Where it occurs, it most often takes the form of idiosyncratic creations that are distinguishable because of their uniqueness, but which, because they did not gain acceptance in any culture, are historically inconsequential (Rouse 1960:313). It is more frequently claimed that an invention occurred in a particular culture because likely prototypes for some new trait can be found in an earlier related culture. Mud-covered baskets, for example, are often argued to be the forerunners of pottery (Arkell 1957). In the majority of cases, however, such proposals remain at the level of speculation.

Similarly, clear-cut evidence of diffusion or migration is frequently lacking in the archeological record. Where substantial changes take place in a short period of time, the prehistorian seeks to discover if these result from the arrival of a new people with an exotic culture, or if the new traits appear as a result of local invention or trait diffusion from somewhere else.

Much of the theoretical literature that discusses how to distinguish between diffusion and independent development has grown out of attempts to provide historical explanations for trait distributions in the absence of archeological evidence. There is general agreement that if a trait has a continuous distribution over a wide area, it probably had a single origin, followed by diffusion. If evidence of the trait is not found outside its present area of diffusion, there is also a tendency to assume that it originated somewhere within that area. Where archeological evidence is lacking, culture historians have tended to assume (much as linguists do about the origin of language families) that, all other factors being equal, a trait probably originated somewhere near the center of its present distribution or else in the area where it presently has the greatest elaboration and complexity. Principles such as these were first enunciated by Edward Sapir (1916) in his paper on *Time Perspective in Ab-*

original American Culture and have since been used by Nelson (1919), Kroeber (1925), Wissler (1926) and many other anthropologists. The principle that older traits generally have wider distributions than more recent ones is now generally recognized as having too many exceptions to be useful (R. B. Dixon 1928:69–72). Likewise, the once popular theory that trait-complexes develop and spread from a common center has been criticized because it ignores the fact that new traits can be added to a complex anywhere throughout its distribution (R. B. Dixon 1928:167–181). In spite of this, there is general agreement that, when used with caution, distributional analyses can produce results of historical value, particularly when traits are analysed one at a time.

Serious disagreements occur when ethnologists attempt to deal with discontinuous trait distributions, and it is in this area that various techniques have been developed which it is claimed can distinguish between diffusion and parallel development. These theories, none of which has ever proved quantifiable, are based for the most part on general and unproved assumptions about the nature of culture and human psychology. Those who believe that different human beings can easily arrive at similar conclusions tend to assume that parallel inventions are common in human history; while those who believe that man is uninventive and that any sort of complex invention is unlikely to be arrived at twice, stress diffusion as the main process underlying culture change. Attempts to evaluate these positions from a psychological point of view have been, and for the most part remain, highly impressionistic.

The first anthropologist to expound the theory of parallel development was Adolf Bastian (Daniel 1963:107; Lowie 1937:30–38). Bastian, who had travelled widely, believed all minds were much alike and concluded that under similar circumstances human beings would arrive at similar solutions for the same problem. As a result, cultural development in different parts of the world tends to follow similar lines, whether or not there is any communication between these regions. De Mortillet had this sort of idea in mind when he proposed his "law of similar development," on the basis of which he argued that the Paleolithic sequence found in France would prove to be a universal sequence of cultural development. The same concept of human nature underlies all unilineal theories of cultural evolution with the exception of that of the Vienna school, which postulates a single line of development producing cultures which then diffused throughout the world (Graebner 1911; Schmidt 1939).

Bastian's view of human nature has been objected to, not because anthropologists disagree with his assumption that human beings are much alike, but because environmental conditions vary from one region to another and the range of alternative cultural solutions for most problems is usually quite broad. Hence, different cultures evolve alternative solutions to the same problem and thereby undergo divergent development.

The more extreme diffusionists have based their work on the assumption that human beings are totally lacking in inventiveness. Innovations are believed to be so rare that even very general traits such as pottery, domestic plants, or mummification can have had only one origin. This concept underlies the work of the Vienna school and that of the "extreme diffusionists" in England during the early part of this century. The latter constructed schemes of culture history which saw all civilization derived from ancient Egypt (G. E. Smith 1915; Perry 1923) or Mesopotamia (Raglan 1939), and believed that all supposedly "advanced traits" (such as mummification, no matter what form it took) could be traced back to a place of origin in one of the ancient civilizations of the Old World (R. B. Dixon 1928:244–264; Daniel 1963:104–127). Vestiges of this sort of thinking can still be found in A. J. Arkell's (1957) claim that pottery was invented only once, or in Munro Edmonson's (1961) attempt to compute a diffusion rate for culture during the Neolithic period by plotting the distance between the points at which traits such as pottery and metal tools are known to appear first in different parts of the world.

One anthropologist who attempted to study human inventiveness was A. L. Kroeber (1948:341–343; 364–367). He observed that many things were not only invented more than once, but that in the scientific field the same discovery was often made within the same year by scientists who had no knowledge of each other's work. This obviously happens because scholars throughout the world are conscious of similar problems and have a common pool of ideas to draw from. Generalizing from this, Kroeber postulated that the more two cultures are alike, and the more their needs are the same, the more likely they are to come up with similar solutions to the same problems. The initial similarities, however, can arise from different sources. Two cultures can be alike because they spring from a common source, and, under these conditions, similar inventions merely help to offset the differences that inevitably must arise as a result of separate development. On the other hand, similarities can develop in historically unrelated cultures that have a similar general adaptation to their environment. Formal similarities can thus result from historical interconnections, functional similarities, and finally from similar cultures (for either of the two reasons given above) generating further similar inventions. In order to distinguish which of these factors is at work in a given situation it is necessary to have either detailed historical information or a highly sophisticated understanding of the nature of culture change. In most situations where historical reconstructions are attempted, the information in neither category is adequate to produce fully satisfactory results. All too often in the past, anthropologists have tried to supplement a lack of historical information with theories of culture that would allow them to reconstruct the past from present day distributional evidence alone. In the next section I will discuss why most of these efforts have proved futile.

The Weakness of the "Culture Historical" Approach

Many debates about historical connections have centered on the nature of the evidence that is needed to prove that similar traits in two cultures are historically related. Graebner argued that the probability of traits found in different areas being historically related varies according to the resemblances in form and function that they exhibit (which are not simply in the nature of the phenomenon) and also according to the number of such traits that the regions involved can be found to have in common. He called these his criteria of "quality" and "quantity." While few ethnologists would deny the general validity of these principles, there is much disagreement as to the way they can be applied. It is sometimes argued, for example, that a large number of similar traits, although not proven to be of common origin, create as great a probability of historical connections between two cultures as do close resemblances in a small number of items.

Ethnologists usually begin by trying to discover whether or not similar traits in two or more cultures are genetically related (that is, derived from a common source), rather than by trying to prove independent invention. One basic assumption, contained in Graebner's criteria of quality, is that the more complex an item of culture is, the greater is the chance of being able to prove common origin. The literature is full of comments to the effect that a particular sort of object is too complicated to have been invented twice. These statements, however, almost invariably turn out to be personal judgments, with little in the way of scientific theory or a reliable estimate of probability to support them. The result is that objects that one anthropologist believes are related, are considered by another not to be. At present, clear-cut decisions are possible only in a limited number of cases, and these are determined largely by the nature of the evidence being considered.

Some objects found in two or more cultures may be shown not only to be "genetically" related but to be products of the same culture. In the recipient cultures these objects are usually called "trade goods," regardless of the means by which they passed from one culture to another. Such objects can usually be distinguished from indigenous material through differences in form and manufacture and also by the fact that they lack historical antecedents in the local culture. No one doubts, for example, that the Roman coins or Central Asian Buddhas that are found in archeological sites in Scandinavia are trade goods (Stenberger *nd;* 124–130). Such objects are similar in every way to other examples known to be of foreign origin and there are no stylistic or technological antecedents in Swedish culture that could account for such a perfect parallelism in design and workmanship. The presence of the same kind of trade goods in two cultures demonstrates contact (however indirect) between them, and this strengthens the chances that ideas could have been exchanged as well as objects. Trade goods thus provide evidence of the existence of channels of communication that can be used to argue the possibility of cultural diffusion.

Zoologists, likewise, may show that domestic plants or animals are not indigenous to certain areas, since the wild species that gave rise to them do not, and probably never did, occur there (McCall 1964:91–101). The genetic constitution of plants and animals frequently constitutes an effective means of distinguishing varieties that share a common origin from those that are the result of parallel development. Moreover, the genetic relationship between tame plants and animals and their wild ancestors provides evidence of their place of origin. The absence of both native wild goats and ancestral forms of wheat or barley in North Africa in post-Pleistocene times indicates, for example, that these items must have been brought into this area, probably in domestic form, from Southwest Asia (Reed 1960:130–134). Plant and animal studies, like trade goods, produce irrefutable evidence of contacts between different regions and, thus, are useful for demonstrating the possibility that traits could have diffused along the same routes. Care is needed, however, not to generalize indiscriminately on the basis of such evidence.

In order to demonstrate historical connections, one must first eliminate the possibility that the similarities in the items being compared are in fact products of convergent development. For many years, diffusionists argued that all pyramidal structures had their origins in ancient Egypt. The fact that the Egyptian pyramids were tombs covering the graves of kings, while the Mesopotamian ziggurats were platforms supporting the temples of important deities did not deter such speculation. It was assumed that whatever differences, in form and function, were found among pyramidal structures in different parts of the world, were the result of divergent development and that all these structures could be traced back to a common prototype. Since that time, archeologists have shown that the Egyptian pyramid developed from the mounds of sand that were originally used to cover individual graves. These developed into an elaborate sun symbol, which in functional—although perhaps no longer in conceptual—terms served the same purpose. The ziggurat, on the other hand, appears to have been an elaboration of the low platforms used (and still used) in southern Iraq to raise houses and public buildings above the level of the river. Far from being the result of divergence from a common prototype, any similarities between the Egyptian pyramid and the Mesopotamian. ziggurat appear to be the result of historically unrelated convergent development from totally different origins.

Once upon a time it was believed that similarities in social organization were indications of widespread historical connections. Morgan (1871:387), for example, argued that since many North American Indian tribes have the same general system of kinship system as have the Tamils in southern India, both groups were historically related. It is clear, however, that since social organization is limited in its variations and is highly correlated with economic organization, it is often convergent in its evolution. No one would argue that since the Nyoro of Central Africa have an Omaha kinship system, they are historically related to the Winnebago of the United States, or would even suggest that the idea of the state had a single origin. Mere typological similarities in social or political organization are no proof of an historical relationship among different groups.

Languages provide an even more instructive example of the lack of historical significance that can be attributed to structural similarities. In the last century it was often argued that typological or structural similarities between languages were indications of historical relationship. Today, it is clear that tone languages have evolved independently in Africa and the Far East and that sex gender is no proof that the Khoisan (Bushman) and Indo-European languages are historically related. Demonstrably related languages, such as those of the Indo-European family, display a wide variety of structural variation, from Latin, which is essentially a synthetic language, to English, which is essentially analytic.

Such structural principles are poor evidence of historical relationships among languages, because types are limited in number and therefore the possibility of convergence is high. Much more reliable proofs of historical relationships can be found in those features of language in which chances of arbitrary association play a significantly greater role. Each word or morpheme (except perhaps for the words "mother" and "father" (Murdock 1959b) is a completely arbitrary association of sound and meaning. In any two vocabularies a linguist expects that no more than four percent of the words will share the same association of form and meaning because of coincidence. Any greater degree of similarity indicates either that words have been borrowed between these two languages or that they share a common origin. According to Greenberg (1957:39–40), an examination of the core vocabulary of the languages involved, and a comparison of the degree to which linguistic similarities between two languages are shared with others that are equally related, will allow the linguist to distinguish the latter kind of relationship from the former. Proof of either sort of historical relationship between languages thus depends not on structural similarities but on a significant number of arbitrary associations between form and meaning.

Unfortunately, in the nonlinguistic domains of culture it is frequently impossible to estimate how arbitrary a trait is and what is the likelihood that the same form could have evolved independently several times. We frequently do not have enough understanding about the behavior of culture to apply Graebner's criteria of quality and quantity intelligently. It is even far from clear, in many cases, to what degree these criteria are distinct. The margin of doubt concerning whether similarities are due to convergence or diffusion is therefore frequently very great.

Applying the criterion of quality, one expects that the more resemblances there are between traits from different cultures, the greater is the chance that they are derived from a common historical source. It has become apparent that general categories, such as pottery or mummification, are meaningless units of comparison, since they cover broad areas of culture and often share few similarities in content. They are, therefore, extremely susceptible to multiple invention. Comparisons must consider specific traits or a complex of closely related traits.

The first task is to determine whether traits that look alike, really are. Just as in linguistics, meaningful lexical comparisons are based on words similar in sound and meaning, so with culture: the categories being compared should be alike both in form and function (Steward and Setzler 1938). Form and function are possibly less arbitrary, yet vary with respect to each other more in the field of culture than they do in linguistics. Hence, the possibility of disparate origins and "false convergence" should be investigated, when any category is found whose members lack a one-to-one correlation in these two (Steward 1929). For example, through a careful analysis of the wear patterns on 300 so-called "celts," J. Sonnenfeld (1962) found that these objects had been put to very different uses in different cultures. Moreover, in this instance, he found no evidence of a significant correlation between form and function. The analysis of the function of a trait, in the sense of both its technological use and its role in the culture as a whole, should be carried out, wherever possible, independently of form so that these two categories of information can later be compared.

It is also obvious that, to constitute satisfactory evidence of a historical relationship, the traits being compared should be nonfunctional. Arrowheads are manufactured out of only a few materials and have a limited number of shapes; hence, it is not inconceivable that various combinations of these attributes have been reinvented many times. Some functions, particularly technological ones, can be determined fairly easily; others are more subtle and it would be folly to pretend that the present state of anthropology can take account of all of them. For example, little is understood about such relationships as those between art styles and social structure, which require a more sophisticated understanding of psychological mediations than is possible at present. For this reason, it is not always possible to distinguish functional and nonfunctional criteria.

Various studies indicate that the possibility of convergent development of elaborate trait-complexes, is greater than common sense would lead one to believe. Therefore, complex similarities in related traits do not necessarily indicate a historical relationship between two cultures.

In 1913, Alexander Goldenweiser enunciated his "principle of limited possibilities" which proposed that parallel and convergent developments are likely to occur for two reasons. The first reason was the usual psychological one, namely, that the range of human reactions to similar problems is frequently limited; hence the chances of the same trait being invented more than once are quite high. The second reason was modelled after the biological concept of selection. It proposed that since the range of traits that any one culture may be able to integrate successfully is limited, features that are different to begin with, often end up being channelled along similar lines. Just as natural selection causes animals having very different origins (such as bats and birds) but occupying similar ecological niches to develop along similar lines, so cultural traits that are different in origin may grow alike if they find themselves in a similar cultural environment. Since anthropologists, unlike biologists, usually are unable to distinguish similarities resulting from convergent development from ones that indicate common origin, they are often unable, from analysis of form and function alone, to determine which of these two factors has been at work.

The principle of limited possibilities is the basis of Rands and Riley's (Riley 1952; Rands 1961) concept of pattern elaboration. These men argue that most innovations are extensions of previously existing patterns, rather than creations along completely new lines. Hence the choices among various alternatives that have been made at any one period will tend to restrict the range of choices that are possible later. Once the nucleus of a complex has been established through a set of primary choices, later traits will tend to develop sequentially from it. Rands and Riley (1958) have illustrated this concept with a comparison of the methods of torture employed by the Iroquois, Aztecs, and Tupinamba (the latter a Brasilian tribe). This complex is analysed by breaking it into component traits on varying levels of generality. The authors conclude that many of the detailed similarities in ritual and technique found in the methods of torture employed by these three groups may be convergent elaborations of a limited number of more general traits that may or may not be historically related. Hence, limitations of choice, as well as functional necessity, may be a factor promoting convergence and thus helping to increase the difficulty of determining whether or not similar traits are historically related.

In a paper discussing two similar games of chance, the first an Aztec, the second a Hindu one, Charles Erasmus (1950) has argued that is is impossible to use probability theory to estimate the likelihood of diffusion as opposed to independent development. In particular, this argument is directed against Tylor's (1879) suggestion that the probability of the recurrent invention of an item of culture varies inversely with the number of common elements that are involved in the complex. In order to apply Tylor's formula one would have to know (1) the exact number of possible alternative combinations that each element in these two games has, (2) all of the opportunities for their combination, and (3) that each of these elements is independent of the others, in the sense that the occurrence of one does not bias the probability of the occurrence of any of the others. The growing understanding of limited possibilities and of pattern elaboration emphasizes how difficult it would be to satisfy the last of these requirements.

Graebner's second criterion, that of quantity, proposes that the greater is the number of qualitative resemblances between two areas, the greater is the chance of there being an historical connection between them. The traits being compared ideally should be independent of each other, if each is to constitute a separate piece of evidence. It is frequently difficult, however, to determine if traits are, in fact, independent. Royal brother-sister marriages, retainer burials, the restriction of gold for the use of the upper classes, and the employment of dwarfs as household servants may be considered as individual traits or as part of a pattern related to a highly stratified society. Since it is difficult to determine whether the elements being compared are truly independent, the same problems that beset the statistical use of quantitative evidence burden the use of qualitative evidence. In fact, it becomes impossible to separate these two categories of data.

In addition to accepting interrelated traits as independent evidence of a historical relationship, there is also frequently a tendency to ignore the relative significance and validity of the individual relationships being proposed and to concentrate mainly on the number. The basic assumption seems to be that if enough similarities are discovered, a few mistaken ones will not greatly bias the evidence. This of course is fallacious. The significance of no item that is used in a quantitative argument is any greater than its individual qualitative value as established in terms of the criteria stated above.

Moreover, when culture areas are being compared, there is all too frequently a tendency to compare traits collected from different cultures within the area and even from different periods. It is argued that proof of historical connections need not depend on detailed comparisons between individual cultures, since traits probably diffused between the two areas gradually and over different routes. Statistically, however, by increasing the number of cultures that traits are selected from, one naturally increases the probability of finding cultural parallels and the value of the evidence is thereby diminished. Rowe (1966) has recently compiled a list of 60 traits common to the Andean and ancient Mediterranean civilizations in order to illustrate the danger of assuming that even a large number of casual similarities between two remote regions is proof of a historical connection between them. Taken individually, and subjected to careful scrutiny in terms of the criteria we have discussed, scarcely any of these traits would escape elimination. They are either too general, too obviously functional, or too interdependent. Considering the vast array of cultures involved and the nature of the traits, any that are not eliminated using these criteria could easily be attributed to chance. Evidence that one plant of Peruvian origin, such as the potato, was known in Europe prior to 1492 would constitute infinitely better evidence of a historical connection between these two areas than do 60 doubtful traits.

A final criterion, often employed in distinguishing between diffusion and independent development, is the ease of communication between the regions involved. Graebner called this the criterion of continuity. While distance and the nature of the terrain undoubtedly affect communication, it is not easy to estimate the effect that these factors have on diffusion, since many cultural variables intervene. Estimates of the ability or desire of ancient peoples to travel frequently vary. An illustration of this is the recent dispute between Sharp (1957) and Suggs (1960) concerning the ability of the Polynesians to use astronomical sightings to chart courses across long stretches of the Pacific Ocean. The notion of routes also causes difficulties. R. B. Dixon (1928:231) argued that it would be unlikely for various traits to have diffused from Southeast Asia to the tropical regions of the New World, since they would have been forgotten during their bearers' long sojourn in the intervening Arctic and temperate regions. However, if recent suggestions of trans-Pacific connections prior to 1492 (Ekholm 1964) are ever confirmed, the significance of this argument would be greatly diminished.

It is clear, then, that even close formal similarities in traits or trait-complexes do not necessarily indicate a common origin. The limitation of possibilities, through various functional constraints, and the similar needs and nature of man, all conspire to make repeated invention, parallel development, and convergence not only possible, but fairly common. When two cultures share many specific, seemingly nonfunctional traits, it seems logical to postulate some sort of historical relationship between them, just as when two languages contain many words with similar sounds and meanings, it is possible to infer some sort of historical relationship between them, either genetic or diffusionary. When dealing with material culture, we must be more cautious, however, since the make-up of few items of culture is not functionally determined, or at least influenced, in some way. Sometimes, historical relationships can be demonstrated by discovering artifacts in one culture which can be demonstrated to be local limitations of objects originally manufactured in another. An example is the crude, but detailed, imitations of Greek coins found in the La Tene culture of western Europe (Powell 1958:100–102). Even so, without the perspective that only archeology can provide, it is often impossible to tell whether close similarities, even between nearby cultures, are the result of their divergence from a common ancestor, the convergence of two originally different cultures, or a combination of both. We have already seen in our discussion of pyramids that, in the absence of archeological evidence, very wrong conclusions may be reached, but once such evidence becomes available, the answers to most problems concerning the types of artifacts that are preserved in the archeological record are quickly forthcoming. These, in turn, provide the basis for a reasonable discussion of the history of those items of culture that have not been preserved.

It was suggested not long ago that proof of diffusion or independent development does not rest on archeological evidence but rather on "a set of theoretical principles that must be objectively applied to each case" (Meggers 1964:522). Linguistics has almost reached the point where this is possible. When dealing with other areas of culture and with artifacts, however, present theories are clearly insufficient to allow us to reconstruct the past using ethnological evidence alone. Solid inferences must be based on archeological evidence, which, if it is sufficient, may allow us to distinguish between the alternative hypotheses that the study of trait distributions raises. Moreover, the further we move into the past the more completely we must rely on purely archeological evidence.

What are the criteria that can be used to determine whether similar objects in noncontiguous cultures are historically related?

(1) It must be demonstrated that the objects or traits in question are genuinely similar in form and function and have enough nonfunctional criteria in common to at least suggest that the similarities between them are likely to result from a common origin. Occasionally, a particular trait or trait-complex is sufficiently unique that its very nature demonstrates an historical relationship. No one doubts that maize or tobacco came from the New World or that the English spoken by the inhabitants of Bombay is of British origin. Most traits, however, are not clear-cut.

(2) Where proof of diffusion seems likely, it must be shown next that the objects that appear to share a common origin are not the products of convergent evolution. To answer this question, detailed archeological data are required concerning the historical antecedents of the objects in question in the various cultures in which they are found. We have already noted how archeological evidence shows that the Egyptian and Mesopotamian "pyramids" developed from entirely different, and historically unrelated, antecedents. Historical analysis also shows that certain highly stylized Mayan motifs, which G. Elliot Smith (1924) claimed were the heads of elephants (and hence were evidence of Hindu influence in Mayan culture), were in fact curvilinear stylizations of the head and bill of a native parrot. Archeological evidence, by allowing prehistorians to trace the local antecedents of various traits, makes a valuable contribution toward distinguishing traits that are genetically related from those that result from convergence.

(3) It is fair to presume that whenever a trait capable of surviving in the archeological record diffused from one area to another over land, it left traces of its passing along the way. Hence, even if a trait now has a discontinous distribution, it should be possible to prove archeologically that at some period its distribution was not discontinuous. This evidence should take the form of a series of archeological sites, which either marks the route along which the trait moved or else shows its former distribution to have embraced the gaps between the regions of its present occurrence (Rouse 1958). The sites within this area should be dated so that one can discover where the trait originated and how it spread. If, for example, a trait turns out to be older at two ends of its total distribution than it is in the middle, the archeological evidence would favor multiple origins with an overlapping distribution rather than a single origin. The same test might profitably be applied to traits with presently continuous distribution, a few of which may turn out to have had more than one origin. It is obvious that it is impossible to find any archeological evidence for many traits, and for others the evidence will be very scanty. In these cases, proof of historical connections cannot be ascertained. Nevertheless, if archeological evidence of historical connections between two areas is forthcoming, then the possibility is enhanced that various other traits, of which no archeological evidence remains, may have had the same history. It is also clear that, even when we are dealing with ethnographic traits that undoubtedly share a common origin, only archeological evidence can demonstrate at what period and by what route they diffused.

(4) When intervening areas are not susceptible to archeological investigation (as is the case in Polynesia where islands are separated by vast stretches of ocean) the argument that similar traits are genetically related must rest largely on the proof of the historical relatedness of traits, such as languages and crops, whose nature is such as to permit no doubt of their common origin. The fact that a Malayo-Polynesian language is spoken on Easter Island, and that typical Polynesian crops are grown there, is infinitely better proof of the close historical relations between that island and the rest of Polynesia than Heyerdhal's reed boats and stonework are proof of an historical connection with South America. The genetic relationship of the former traits is assured but the genetic relationship of the ones listed by Heyerdhal is only a matter of conjecture.

Distinguishing Diffusion and Migration

Various criteria have been established to help to distinguish pure trait diffusions from cultural changes brought about by movements of people. Most of these criteria are designed to pinpoint major discontinuities resulting from the total replacement of one population by another. This kind of treatment, as we have noted before, ignores the fact that movements of people and traits at times take place quite independently of each other, and consequently disregards the variety of situations in which movements of population and of cultural traits can and do occur. In 1939, W. M. Flinders Petrie (p. 9) listed nine types of culture change (excluding independent invention) all but one of which involved migrations of people. Although this list reflects a rather melodramatic view of culture change, it has the merit of recognizing the wide variety of circumstances under which culture change can come about. Its categories include: (1) general substitution of population, (2) killing the men and scattering the women, (3) killing the men and capturing the women, (4) enslaving the men and taking the women, (5) victors ruling over slaves, (6) victors ruling over stable populations, (7) mixture of diverse peoples, (8) assimilation of immigrants, and (9) merely the adoption of foreign ideas. Another list, anthropologically more sophisticated, was drawn up by Eoin MacWhite in 1956. It distinguished between various types of organized invasions, casual immigration, and the different ways trait diffusion (acculturation) can come about through raiders, foreign visitors, or local groups being in contact with neighboring cultures. These lists differ from the one below in that they treat the entire problem from the point of view of culture change and fail to include instances where changes in population took place with little or no corresponding change in material culture. From the point of view of human history, population movements of the latter sort are as significant as the ones that bring about major cultural changes. The particular categories we discuss are obviously points on a continuum, and not a set of rigidly defined situations.

I. The first kind of change is the total replacement of one population and their culture by another. Normally, a change of this sort involves one group driving out another and occupying its former homeland. This probably happens most frequently between adjacent and culturally similar groups and under these conditions "culture change" (as opposed to population change) is minimal. When the invaders are culturally different from their predecessors, the break is usually quite apparent in the archeological record and where distinct populations are involved there may even be a noticeable discontinuity in physical type. While total changeovers of this sort are relatively rare, one would think they could be detected easily in the archeological record. Such, however, is not always the case.

To begin with, one must be certain that the sharp break in the cultural continuity of the archeological record is real and not merely apparent. Evidence from one site or from only a small area may not adequately reflect what has happened elsewhere. Thus, the first task of the archeologist is to determine that the discontinuity he has noted holds true in terms of the whole culture. Secondly, he must determine that the total sequence has been recovered and that no period has been overlooked. It is possible that for ecological reasons, or perhaps because of unstable political conditions, a region was abandoned for a time before a new population moved in or the old one returned. The failure to note this temporal gap could result in a misunderstanding of the relationship between the cultures occupying the region before and afterwards and might even result in interpreting the same local tradition at two stages in its development as being two unrelated cultures. Such problems can be reduced to a minimum by extensive excavations and a careful study of the stratigraphic and chronological evidence. Finally, the archeologist must examine the content of the cultures he is studying as thoroughly as possible. You may recall that archeologists in Nubia failed to see the historical relationship between the Meroitic and Ballana cultures, because they concentrated on burials and tomb types, the particular area of culture where the greatest discontinuity existed.

Secondly, whenever it is possible to do so, it must be demonstrated that there was a genuine change in population. This requires evidence that the previous population was abruptly replaced by a new one. Where racial differences are noted between the skeletons associated with the two cultures, it must be shown that the change in physical type took place abruptly and at the same time the change in culture came about. Evidence of only a gradual change in physical type would, of course, weaken the argument that a total (or almost total) replacement of population took place.

Thirdly, something must be found out about the nature of the replacement. Often, the clues will consist of evidence of widespread destruction, followed by the settlement of people with a different culture. This evidence must be more convincing than the small collection of apparently unburied bodies that Mortimer Wheeler has suggested indicates that the Indus Valley city of Mohenjodaro was sacked (Dales 1964). The documentation of how replacement took place requires extensive and carefully controlled excavations, and it appears that the archeological record for few cultures is equal to this task.

As further proof of the intrusive nature of the new culture, the archeologist not only must demonstrate that it suddenly replaced an older one, but, must also show where and from what antecedents the intrusive culture developed. In short, the new culture must be shown to be native to another region. This requirement rules out attempts to attribute the origins of "new" cultures to unknown regions.

This is particularly important in Northeast Africa where little archeological work has been done outside the Nile Valley, and where many a hypothetical antecedent of some Nile Valley culture is said to exist in some region that is archeologically unknown. While no prehistorian must be denied the right to controlled speculation, the tendency of some scholars to pile one unsubstantiated hypothesis on another, often to the point where they ignore meaningful evidence close at hand, has incited a rather positivistic reaction among their less romantic colleagues.

Finally, Rouse (1958) is correct in suggesting that the route of any migration should be worked out and the distribution of all the sites checked to see if the resulting pattern makes sense historically. Furthermore, the archeologist should attempt to find out if environmental and cultural conditions would have permitted a migration to take place. Such environmental factors are especially important in ecologically marginal regions, such as North Africa, where there have been considerable variations in climate.

The difficulties that replacement hypotheses can run into when there is a lack of detailed archeological data are demonstrated by the recent questions raised concerning the validity of the "Neanderthal hypothesis" (Brace 1964; Coon 1965:52, 53). For a long time, many physical anthropologists believed that the Classic Neanderthal men of western Europe differed radically from Homo sapiens, perhaps even constituting a separate species of hominid. Although relatively few skeletons had been found, and few sites were excavated that belonged to the transitional period, it was widely accepted that Neanderthal man, along with his Mousterian culture had been swept aside between 30,000 and 40,000 years ago by modern Homo sapiens. It was assumed that these latter types, coming from the east, brought with them the earliest Upper Paleolithic [blade] cultures found in Europe. Even those who did not consider the Classic Neanderthals to be a separate species, saw them as being brushed aside, much as the North American Indians were by the Europeans, with only a few of their racial traits managing to survive in a very diluted form in remote regions.

Today this theory is being widely challenged. It has been suggested not only that the Classic Neanderthals of western Europe may have evolved into Homo sapiens in that area (aided perhaps by genetic drift from other regions), but also that the Mousterian culture evolved of its own accord into the Upper Paleolithic Perigordian I culture of western Europe. Once the theoretical issue is framed in this way, the current lack of archeological data becomes evident, since it renders virtually impossible any final solution of this problem at this time.

II. The second type of culture change is that resulting from the movement of an organized group of people into a new area. Such groups settle down alongside the native population, as conquerors and rulers—as the Tussi were in Ruanda (Murdock 1959a:350; Willey 1953a); as subjects of the native population—as bedouin groups from Palestine and Arabia often were in ancient Egypt; or else they interact with the local population on a basis of equality. Under these conditions, the incoming group may preserve its sense of ethnic identity and much of its own culture for a long time. Eventually, however, the old and the new cultures blend and may produce a single culture made up of various traits from each of the ancestral ones. In general, the relative importance of the contribution made by the two cultures will depend on the size and importance of the groups involved as well as the degree to which the incoming culture is adapted to its new environment. Various factors, such as the desire of the dominant minority group to preserve their sense of identity vis-à-vis their subjects, may impede the total blending of the two cultures. Special situations may also produce highly distorted forms of cultural blending. If, for example, large numbers of men from a particular tribe are killed in war and the women of the tribe marry outsiders, various traits from the old culture that are associated with women will be more likely to survive than those associated with men. An example of this, is reported in the Lesser Antilles, where the Caribs are said to have killed off the Arawak men, but married the women (Rouse 1964:502). While the Caribs adopted the Arawak language, their arrival appears to have terminated the relatively elaborate, priestly religion of earlier times which centered on the worship of deities known as *zemis*. In this instance, cultural merging could be expected to take place quite rapidly.

In these situations the problem of proof is even more difficult than it is with total replacements. At one time there was a tendency to attribute almost every change in culture to the intrusion of some new groups or "master race" (Daniel 1963:104–127, 139–153). Unfortunately, using this model of culture change uncritically, almost any new trait can be attributed to the intrusion of a new group, while cultural continuities in the same culture can be ascribed to the survival of the native population. Thus, this sort of explanation can be read into almost every example of cultural change that is found in the archeological record. To avoid unbridled speculation, strict rules are needed to govern such interpretations. The purpose of these rules—which are simply a modification of the ones required to prove total replacement—is to help the prehistorian to distinguish culture change that really does result from the arrival of new populations from changes that come about as a result of internal developments or trait diffusion.

In order to demonstrate that the innovations observed in the archeological record were brought in by an organized migration, sites belonging to the intrusive culture associated with this group must be found and dated to the period when, or just before, the new traits became general in the local culture. These sites must be shown to belong not only to a culture that is different from contemporary cultures in the area, but also one for which a homeland and place of origin can be located elsewhere. In addition, the route of the migration must be found, its direction traced, and conditions shown to be such as to permit a migration over the route proposed (Rouse 1958). Finally, it must be shown that the culture is genuinely intrusive, in the sense of permanently occupying the region. In the seventeenth century, hunting bands from Northern Ontario frequently spent the winter living in encampments outside Huron villages, where they traded dried meat and skins for corn meal. This interaction between the Huron and Algonkians may have introduced various items of Algonkian culture to their hosts, but their settlement in Huronia was merely part of their annual cycle and did not result in any permanent Algonkian settlement in this region. Proof of population movement requires a demonstration that the incoming groups actually settled in the region (which may be done in part by showing that their settlements were permanent ones) and that they and their culture gradually mingled with the indigenous one. This in turn, requires archeological evidence of the gradual mingling of cultural traits over time and (assuming that the intrusive groups were different to begin with) physical anthropological evidence showing genetic mingling.

Clearly, it is sufficiently difficult to satisfy these criteria so that certain instances of major culture change resulting from the blending of two groups (especially when this went on quickly and, therefore, is hard to detect in the archeological record) are likely to be ruled out for lack of evidence. The validity of this hypothesis can be considerably reduced, however, if, as more archeological data accumulate, it can be demonstrated that the individual traits that were assumed to be brought in by the intrusive culture (and hence all at one time) actually appear in the archeological record at different times. This is often the case. It is felt by many prehistorians that it is better to have criteria that are sufficiently strict so that certain (apparently) good cases are ruled out for lack of evidence, rather than to have rules so loose that any instance of culture change can be interpreted as being of this type. The logic behind this is that situations where proof of membership in this category is not forthcoming fall into a recognizable residual category. Later, when more evidence is available, they may be restudied and assigned to this one. Confusion reigns when none of the categories being used is clearly recognizable as a residual one.

III. A third type of change involves the organized migration of large numbers of people, but is characterized by little cultural change in the region they enter (at least of a sort that is detected in the archeological record). In these instances the intrusive population accepts the material culture of the area it moves into. This can occur either because the group moves rapidly and carries little of its own culture along with it, or because the area into which it moves is ecologically different from the one it left and its old culture is unsuited to the new conditions. It can also happen where the culture of the new area is considered by the migrants to have greater prestige than their own. When nomads, such as the Hebrews, settled in Palestine, they quickly adopted the material culture of the farming and urban groups who already lived in the area. Likewise, the Philistines, who settled in the Canaanite cities along the coast, after what appears to have been a rapid flight from their original homeland, adopted the native culture of the region so completely that only a new style of tomb and a few artistic motifs can presently be used to distinguish them from the original population (Kenyon 1960:221–239). To the archeologist who has no knowledge of historical records, the archeological evidence, consisting mostly of towns pillaged by the invaders and later rebuilt in much the same style as before, would probably be insufficient to suggest that important ethnic and linguistic changes had taken place. Similarly, the Germanic invasions of much of the western Roman Empire led to such a swift adoption of Latin culture by them that the period of invasion might easily appear in the archeological record as merely one of political instability and cultural decline, rather than as a period that also saw considerable movements of population.

Clues that suggest the intrusion of organized groups are signs of war, cultural decline, and fairly rapid cultural change, the latter being induced, in part by the decline in culture and in part by social and cultural innovations introduced by the intruders. This sort of evidence is rarely sufficient, by itself, to prove that new groups settled in the region. Evidence of rapid changes in physical type may increase the probability of migration, but here again caution must be exercised against unwarranted speculation based on inadequate data. Archeological evidence of intrusion may be found in the form of the temporary camps and settlements of the invaders prior to acculturation. These sites are probably scarce and difficult to identify. It seems more difficult to find evidence of this sort of change than to find evidence of types I and II. The evidence is also often more ambiguous and difficult to interpret, since it is hard to tell the difference between the sites of an intrusive mobile population and those of groups of raiders who merely passed through a region.

In some cases, the intrusive population may adopt the local material culture, yet impose its own language on the region. In such instances, lexicostatistical data may reveal when a particular speech community underwent expansion and thus may provide clues concerning population movements. Such evidence, along with historical accounts, suggests that the Nubian-speaking peoples arrived in the Nile Valley from the southwest sometime during the Ballana period, although there are few indications of cultural discontinuity at this time. Apparently, they adopted the culture of the region and yet arrived in sufficient numbers to replace the earlier local language, Meroitic (Trigger 1966a). A similar situation seems to hold with the arrival of the Greeks in Crete, an event that appears to have preceded rather than brought about the collapse of Minoan culture. Commenting on this situation, Fritz Schachermeyr has observed:

> It is a great mistake to assume that historical events are always reflected in the archaeological record of stylistic phases. Many historical upheavals occurred without leaving any such traces behind them (Palmer 1965:180–181).

The absence of linguistic evidence does not, of course, prove that population movements never occurred, since the intrusive people may have adopted the language as well as the material culture of the region into which they moved.

IV. A fourth type of culture change is that resulting from an influx of outsiders who do not enter a culture as an organized group, but rather as individuals or families who find a place for themselves within the existing social order. These people may come as settlers, refugees, missionaries, slaves, or as the foreign husbands or wives of members of the indigenous group. Some may acculturate very quickly, others, for religious or other social or cultural reasons, may seek to preserve certain aspects of their old culture within a new social setting. Such people, especially those who possess special skills, can be important agents of diffusion. In Tudor times, the English government offered substantial incentives to foreign craftsmen to induce them to settle in England and teach their skills to English workers (Hodgen 1952:174–176). This is an example of the deliberate encouragement of migration in an effort to effect culture change. When such migrations continue from a single source over a long period of time, they can result in a considerable amount of cultural convergence. The conversion of the northern part of Lower Nubia from Christianity to Islam appears to have come about as more and more Egyptian Moslems bought land in that region and began to settle down and convert their neighbors

(Trigger 1965:149). The main characteristic of this sort of change is that all the various traits being introduced do not appear at the same time, as they do when introduced by population replacements and organized migrations. Moreover, it does not interrupt the essential continuity of the indigenous culture. For this reason, it is extremely difficult for the archeologist to distinguish between this sort of culture change and the results of simple trait diffusion.

Since the newcomers of unorganized migrations are usually absorbed directly into the fabric of the existing society, intrusive sites are not associated with them. Only rarely is it possible to find ghettos made up of numbers of such immigrants, who lived together in order to retain certain aspects of their old way of life. Such situations are hard to distinguish from the results of organized migration and in many ways they represent, socially as well as archeologically, an intermediate type. Even if foreign households can be discovered within communities, it may be difficult to tell whether they belonged to itinerant groups visiting the community or to immigrants who came to live there. Where the native people and the migrants are physically different, the discovery of significant numbers of new skeletal types, and of the gradual mingling of new physical characteristics with those of the local population, may shed light on this problem. While the effect of this sort of migration on the genetic constitution of the population may be significant, the cultural effects are probably little different from those of trait diffusion. Hence, the difficulties of distinguishing the two do not create a serious problem. Moreover, the more massive the migration is, the greater is the chance the prehistorian will be able to detect it. Thus, the chance of noting this kind of change tends to vary more or less directly in proportion to its historical importance.

V. Unorganized migrations take place that have no marked effect on the recipient culture. Under these circumstances, the immigrant accepts the general culture of the society into which he is moving. This normally happens if he believes the latter culture to be more desirable than the one he has left. Unskilled prisoners, slaves, or migrant laborers are unlikely to possess any special skills that they can transmit to such a culture. At most, they may retain some of their old beliefs and personal habits and perhaps pass some of these on to their children. This is especially likely to happen if they are alienated from the new society by a sense of inferiority or are refugees forced to flee their native land but still sentimentally attached to it.

While movement from society to society, both forced and voluntary, is characteristic of complex societies, it is not unknown in primitive ones. Occasionally, it can take place on a large scale and yet leave little imprint on the recipient culture. Among the Iroquois, for example, large numbers of prisoners frequently were incorporated into the society of their captors, often so completely that they would refuse repatriation even when the opportunity for it was freely offered to them. From a cultural viewpoint such movements are often of minor importance, but in terms of understanding population dynamics and social organization they are of considerable interest. Unfortunately, it is very difficult to find evidence of such movements, although some work may be done in this direction, either through physical anthropology or through studies of shifts in the overall distribution of population.

VI. Our sixth category is trait diffusion. All culture diffuses as a result of contact between people, but trait diffusion involves no permanent shifts in population. Trait diffusion comes about either as a result of prolonged casual contacts between neighboring groups, or as a result of contacts between specialists such as traders or artisans. The itinerant craftsman, the wandering pilgrim, and the ambassador to a foreign country, all potential instruments of diffusion, do not represent any permanent exchange of population between two groups. Occasionally, the archeologist may discover clear-cut evidence of mechanisms of diffusion, such as the Assyrian trading posts in Anatolia that we have mentioned already. Evidence of contact more often takes the form of trade goods or similar innovations appearing in nearby cultures at approximately the same time. Where traits have continuous distributions, and the possibility of diffusion from a single point of origin is high, it is necessary only to correlate each trait in time and in space in order to show where it originated and in which direction it moved. If the earliest point of occurrence coincides with a region where the trait has obvious cultural prototypes, the chances of it having evolved there are high. Where proof of continuous distribution is not forthcoming, individual traits must be judged according to the criteria set forth above, and some personal decision arrived at regarding the probability of independent development as opposed to common origin. Whenever possible, evidence should be sought concerning the nature of the contacts involved in trait diffusion. Unless they consciously avoid or reject foreign traits, adjacent cultures probably exert a wide range of influences over each other as a result of fairly continuous general contacts. The diffusion of some ideas over long distances may require considerably more specialized mechanisms.

Since all cases of diffusion, for which actual population movements have not been proven, form part of this category, it is in effect a final residual one. Within it, it is frequently impossible to distinguish between trait diffusion that definitely was unaccompanied by population movements of any type and those cases where migration may be involved, but is not proved to be.

VII. The final cause of culture change that must always be considered is independent invention. The problems of distinguishing traits that appear as a result of independent invention from those that appear as a result of diffusion have been discussed above. No further treatment is required here.

Conclusion

We have been examining the various cultural processes associated with movements of people and with the invention and dispersal of cultural traits. Although we have not examined in any great detail the idea of a culture as a functionally integrated system, we have stressed the importance for any sort of historical reconstruction of knowing the role that the various artifacts being studied have played within any particular culture. While the existing cultural system may affect the innovation and acceptance of new traits, this does not prevent us from studying the history of individual traits in their own right. The examination of these traits, both individually and in their cultural setting, provides a basis for making inferences about the processes of cultural change, such as we described in the last section.

We have also seen that even when the prehistorian makes full use of all the archeological, physical anthropological, and linguistic data at his disposal, he is still often unable to discern all of the historical factors that have shaped cultural change. The reliability of deductive explanations, based on general theories of the nature of culture, is very low. Reliable explanations are only possible if we have detailed archeological (both cultural and physical) and linguistic data. The solution to most problems requires increasingly refined local chronologies and the detailed investigation of the culture history of adjacent regions. The archeological recovery and analysis of cultural and skeletal data is slow, painstaking work, but it is the basis on which most of the progress in prehistoric studies is built. The interpretation of this evidence is enhanced by a growing understanding of the nature of culture change, by the prehistorian's awareness of theoretical developments in the fields of ethnology and social anthropology, and by the creative application of these findings to the interpretation of the archeological record. These problems of interpretation constitute the true theoretical domain of prehistory and represent a range of skills different from, but at least as extensive, as those that must be possessed by the field archeologist.

5

Social Development

I N THE LAST CHAPTER we discussed factors that promote changes both in culture and in populations. In particular, we discussed the ways in which cultures are modified, and sometimes overwhelmed, by these processes. In this chapter we wish to view prehistory in terms not of various culture traits but of ongoing social systems. The necessity for each generation to be socialized by the generation that precedes it assures a continuity in society even when social institutions may be in the throes of rapid change. Social systems thus constitute the matrix for culture change inasmuch as all changes in the ideas and behavior of groups come about as a result of the experiences of individuals within society. The matrix is not constant, however, but is itself a product of culture; hence, alterations in the economic substructure or the value systems of society can bring about changes in patterns of social and political relations. Such changes either may be deliberate—such as a tribe consciously adopting a new rule concerning incest (Pospisil 1958)—or they may represent unplanned and largely ad hoc responses to new conditions.

We already have suggested that types of kinship systems and political organization are limited in number and, because of the frequency of convergent development, are poor indicators of historical relationships Murdock (1949:20; 1945; 1959c:134) and others have shown that this convergence comes about because only a few basic configurations of social relations have enough coherence to give them a measure of relative stability. Thus, while social organization is of little use in tracing genetic relationships between cultures, the limitations imposed by functional necessity make it of immense value for reconstructing the prehistory of specific societies. This is because the resulting regularities permit the prehistorian to formulate a large number of fairly dependable inferences about the development of particular institutions. Once the prehistorian is able to determine the general nature of the changes he observes in the archeological record, he can then make specific and highly probable statements concerning the nature of corresponding social and political developments. Through an understanding of such changes in social structure, the record of cultural changes becomes functionally more meaningful.

Inferring Social Structure

The direct inference of social and political organization from archeological evidence is a procedure that is still very underdeveloped although in recent years much valuable work has been done in the field. Chang (1958) has published one study of the relationships between community layouts and clan organization among primitive agriculturalists and another (1962) dealing with hunting and reindeer herding peoples in the arctic. These studies are cross-cultural comparisons of living societies, and have provided interesting statistical correlations between settlement plans and community organization. The archeologist, knowing the settlement plans of the prehistoric communities he is studying, can use these studies to gain an idea of the variety of types of social structure that might have been associated with these groups, as well as the relative probabilities for each. Steward's (1955:122–150) formulations of the economic correlates of patrilineal and composite band structures, if valid, can similarly be used to infer prehistoric band organization in cultures for which the subsistence pattern is known.

Attempts are also being made to reconstruct community organization by analysing the distribution of different types of artifacts within a single component. These studies seek to discover residential divisions within a community using design motifs, or evidence of occupational differences (Deetz 1965; Longacre 1966; Hill 1966). Because of their experimental nature, most of these studies use a direct historical approach, which combines a knowledge of the social and political organization of an area in historic times with archeological evidence in order to infer what these institutions were like at an earlier period. Sanders (1965) has used a similar approach to trace the pattern of city states that existed in the Teotihuacan Valley in sixteenth century Mexico back into earlier times. The direct historical approach seems to be particularly useful in areas such as highland Mexico, the Southwestern United States, the Arctic or in Polynesia where distinct cultural traditions have persisted over long periods of time and where most cultural developments have been of internal origin and appear to be closely correlated with economic changes.

Other efforts are being made to use linguistic data to reconstruct prehistoric kinship systems. On the basis of a comparative study of Indo-European terms, Paul Friedrich (1966) has suggested that the proto-Indo-European kinship system was of the Omaha type[1] and probably was used by patriarchal, patrilocal families living in small houses or adjacent huts located in small, distant, and exogamous villages. Friedrich suggests that this hypothesis, based entirely on linguistic evidence, should be checked against relevant archeological data concerning settlement patterns, and against historical data as far back as it goes.

---

[1] Murdock (1959a:29) defines an Omaha kinship system as one in which "cross-cousins are terminologically differentiated alike from siblings, parallel cousins, and each other, the children of a mother's brother being equated with kinsmen of a higher generation, e.g., being called "uncle" or "mother," whereas a father's sister's children are equated with kinsmen of a lower generation." This system occurs almost exclusively in patrilineal societies.

Reconstructions are also being made on the basis of archeological and historical evidence interpreted in the light of relevant, or presumably relevant, ethnographic data. Zuidema (1964) and Lounsbury, for example, have argued that the social and political organization of the Inca was not unlike that of the present day Bororo and Gê peoples of nearby Brazil, and Coe (1965) has postulated a social organization for the Maya lowlands in ancient times that was based on a periodic rotation of power among four equal segments of the community in a manner structurally similar to that found among the present day Berbers of the Atlas Mountains.

The greatest danger in this sort of work is that of drawing parallels between archeological and ethnological data on the basis of an insufficient sample or without understanding the significance of the ethnographic evidence. Nothing can be more misleading than coming to conclusions based on statistical correlations that seem sound, but having a poor understanding of their structural explanations. For example, in Bororo villages in South America, as in many African ones, houses are arranged in a circle around a central open space. Among the Bororo, the arrangement of houses is by moieties and clans, and, according to Lévi-Strauss (1953:534; 1963:141–142), this arrangement reflects "a model [of social organization] existing consciously in the native mind." In short, the Bororo village is an "objective and crystallized external projection" of an idea. Among the Zulu, doughnut-shaped settlements result from a desire to have a protected cattle enclosure in the centre of the encampment (Murdock 1959a:383). Circular settlement patterns have been found in the Tripolje culture of the Ukraine (fourth millennium B.C.), although they are not the only type of village associated with that culture. A casual comparison might interpret these circular villages in terms of either the Bororo or Zulu model and might be wide of the mark either way. A more systematic approach would survey as many cultures as possible that have doughnut-shaped villages in order to determine all of the factors that tend to produce such villages. The archeologist, for his part, would try to find out more about the function of different parts of the Tripolje village. The soil in the village square could be analysed to see if it had been used as a cattle pen and the distribution of artifacts might be studied house by house to see if there were any special clusterings that would suggest divisions corresponding to those of the Bororo clans. Finally, an effort might be made to see if the two houses in the center of the Tripolje village of Kolomiishchina functioned as men's houses and were similar to those of the Bororo.

A more serious example of unscientific interpretation is the suggestion that the presence of female figurines in a culture constitutes evidence of "matriarchal" social organization (Neustupny 1961:45, 46). There is, as far as I know, no ethnological evidence to support the validity of this correlation. On the other hand, there is a good deal of evidence to show that a tradition of female figurines on which sexual attributes are emphasized, has a wide distribution in Europe and the Near East, beginning in Upper Paleolithic times and persisting into the iron age. These figurines are not associated with any one type of culture but with a broad range of cultures and they appear to have first been made by hunting groups, which generally speaking tend to have patrilineal or bilateral organizations rather than matrilineal ones.

The Origin of Complex Societies

Because of the vast amount of anthropological literature concerning social and political organization, we will restrict the following discussion to certain theoretical problems related to our subsequent examination of Predynastic Egypt. Little will be said about kinship systems in general, mainly because little is known about household and community organization in Egypt in Predynastic times. Indeed, little is known about it even for historic times, despite the abundance of texts and the large amount of archeological data. What is known has been summarized in anthropological terms by G. P. Murdock (1959a:107). The Egyptians apparently had no primary kin terms, except those used to designate members of the nuclear family. More distant relatives were called by terms that either were extensions of nuclear family terms (father and grandfather were called by the same term, *jt*) or else descriptive ones (for example, mother's brother was called *sn·s n mwt·s*, literally, her brother of her mother). Inheritance appears to have been bilateral and there is no evidence of extended families, lineages, sibs, or clans. In the royal family, brother-sister marriage occurred and it appears that even among the lower classes incest taboos did not extend to first cousins. Polygyny and concubinage were common only in official circles and newly married couples established an independent and apparently neolocal residence.

One bit of Victorian romanticism, not yet fully exorcised from the literature, is the idea that the social organization of Egypt in the historic period contained survivals of an earlier matrilineal structure (Murray 1951:100–104; Edwards 1964:31). This suggestion was made at a time when anthropologists were arguing that matrilineal organizations were more primitive than patrilineal ones and had preceded the latter everywhere in the world. Moreover, a certain amount of evidence was found that seemed to confirm it. This evidence included the fact that an individual's mother, but not his father, is sometimes named in ancient Egyptian inscriptions; that marriage contracts frequently make provision for property belonging to a man's wife; and that kings married their sisters, which it was argued suggested that the throne was inherited in the female line. Thus only by marrying his sister could a Pharaoh assure the succession to his son. None of these arguments are very convincing. The naming of mothers rather than fathers may have been a way of distinguishing half-siblings in polygynous families, and the specification of a wife's property is only an indication that women could inherit and retain rights over property (Hughes 1966). Pharaohs, in fact, often did not marry their sisters and, when they did, they were often succeeded by the offspring of less important wives. The mythical charter of kingship, according to which a king succeeds his predecessor in the same way that Horus did his father Osiris, clearly postulates a patrilineal succession. Early Egyptologists, steeped in the evolutionary theories of the time, managed to misinterpret a bilateral kinship structure and the fairly high position of women in Egyptian society as evidence of matriliny. In doing so, they did not err as badly as the Arabicists of the day, who managed to see evidence of matriliny in the patrilineal society of pre-Islamic Arabia.

About community organization even less is known. Scarcely any Predynastic town plans have been published and most of the settlements that have been excavated seem to consist of randomly scattered houses.

A good deal more, however, can be ascertained about the social and political developments that transformed Egypt from a scattering of simple, food-producing villages into a united and civilized state. Understanding this process requires some knowledge of the voluminous literature concerning the origin of complex societies. At present, there is no single theory of their origin, but rather a number of different ones, formulated at different times and by scholars in different fields.

To begin with, some terms must be defined—rather arbitrarily—since frequently there is debate concerning their meaning. There is a tendency to treat studies of the "development of civilization," the "rise of states," and the "growth of urban society" as being more or less synonymous. This is clearly sloppy usage since the terms city, state, and civilization refer to a unit of settlement, a type of political organization, and a level of cultural development respectively. Let us then agree to use the term "complex society" as an overall expression referring to any society characterized by one or more of these features.

By a state is meant any society having at its head a permanently constituted authority which is able to apply coercive measures for the enforcement of its decisions (S. Moore 1960:643). This definition applies not only to dictatorial regimes but to all modern states, as any American who attempts to avoid paying his income tax would soon learn. Authority or leadership is present in one form or another in all societies. In stateless societies, however, the enforcement of decisions rests solely on public opinion, rather than on the coercive forces that are at the disposal of the government. In such societies, decisions are obeyed only in so far as they are pleasing to the parties involved or in so far as the fear of ostracism or group violence compels people to do so. Stateless societies are found among all hunting and gathering peoples and many primitive agriculturalists. Some groups, such as the Plains Indians, had warrior associations or secret societies which had the right to punish tribesmen for breaches of discipline during certain seasons of the year (such as during major hunts that were important for the survival of the group) (Forde 1934: 56–57). This function was not permanent, however, and a band having a society of this kind did not constitute a state. States are invariably socially stratified to some degree, but not all stratified societies are states. Several recognized classes, including slaves, existed among the Natchez, Haida, and Tlingit. Yet in these societies chiefs did not possess the coercive power that would have made them heads of state. In addition to economic surpluses, the existence of a state requires a fairly sedentary population that can be effectively coerced. These requirements are frequently met, however, and states are founded on a wide variety of economies, some of them very elaborate, others having only a simple division of labor.

Although attempts have been made to define cities in terms of size or density of population, the results generally have been unsatisfactory. There are villages in many parts of the world known to contain several thousand inhabitants all of whom are engaged in agriculture or craft production for strictly local use. While many ancient cities, and even some of the traditional ones in West Africa in recent times, contained a large number of farmers (Bascom 1955), the chief criterion of a city is that it comprises a sizable population that is not primarily involved in food production. The medieval European city, although often containing only a few hundred people, was a place where craftsmen and traders lived, who exchanged their exotic and manufactured goods with the farmers of the nearby hinterland in return for food (Weber 1958:65–67). Hence, cities are sometimes defined as communities devoted to manufacture and trade. Unfortunately, this definition is too limited for general use. Cities have also been created as centers of government, religious activity, defense, and even recreation. The traditional Chinese city was a walled administrative center where government officials and local landlords lived. The latter found life in town more interesting than in the country and, by living near the seat of the government, they were better protected against attacks by disgruntled peasants. In addition, these towns attracted large numbers of artisans and retainers, who served the needs of the upper classes. Fei (1953:114–115) has argued that the Chinese city produced only a small amount of goods for sale in the surrounding hinterland.

Cities are found in heavily stratified societies with a complex division of labor. They serve as the nuclei where the specialized activities of such societies are located, be they political, economic, or social. Since cities are very efficient settings for such activities, there appears to be a tendency for increasing social stratification and economic complexity to encourage the development of an urban settlement pattern. On the other hand, at least two early civilizations, those of Old Kingdom Egypt (Frankfort 1956:97–98; Kraeling and Adams 1960:124–164) and the Classic Maya (Coe 1957), do not appear to have had cities. The elite activities of these societies were discharged in a more dispersed setting.

The third of these terms is the most controversial. According to some definitions, a civilization is a segment or cycle in the history of a complex society (Kroeber 1953:275); according to others, it is a term restricted to complex societies that attain particularly high standards of ethical behavior or artistic output, measured against some absolute standard. The latter definitions are particularly objectionable from an anthropological point of view, since in restricting the term (often in practice if not in theory) to complex societies, they appear to deny moral or artistic accomplishments to "primitive" peoples. By and large, the term is used to refer to societies that have reached an advanced level of cultural development. The criteria that are used to define this level include literacy, urbanization, monumental architecture, formal art styles, exact and predictive sciences, as well as the existence of the state (Childe 1950). A particular civilization is normally identified in terms of a loose constellation of these criteria, but sometimes literacy or the presence of cities is felt to be sufficient. Morgan (1907:12), for example, treated the invention of phonetic writing as an "index fossil" of civilization, and Sjoberg (1960:33, 38) has maintained, solely on this basis, the argument that since Old Kingdom Egypt had writing it also must have had cities. These criteria, however, since they are not sufficiently interrelated, cannot be expected to define all societies that are structurally at the same level of development. The Precolumbian Maya had writing but lacked cities, whereas the highland Mexicans had cities but did not have a developed system of writing. Art and monumental architecture are poor indices, not only because they are developed to different degrees in different civilizations, but also because the materials used by some groups are more perishable than those used by others. The

Chinese, who used wood to build most of their public buildings, have left far fewer ancient monuments than have the ancient Egyptians and Greeks, who built in stone. If the term civilization is to be meaningful, it must be defined structurally rather than in terms of the presence or absence of specific items of culture.

Excellence in art, literature, and crafts depends on workers who are well trained and highly specialized. This degree of specialization is not found among the part- or full-time village specialists who serve the needs of whole communities, or among craftsmen who move from place to place selling their wares. Advanced specialization requires a high degree of technical knowledge, the specialization of labor, and patrons who will sponsor such craftsmen and use their products. Civilization can be described as a stage of development which begins when artists, craftsmen, and scholars appear, whose products and services are designed, not for all the members of a community, but rather for high status groups within society. Such a development involves the differentiation of an elite and a folk culture within the same society, and the beginning of the dichotomy between what Redfield (1941; 1947) called a Great and a Little Tradition. Herta Haselberger (1961:341) has made much the same point concerning art, when she notes that societies that are not strongly stratified have homogenous art styles, but in more complex ones, like precontact Hawaii and Benin, it is possible to distinguish a "patrician" and "plebian" tradition.

Civilizations are, by necessity, societies that are socially stratified, and all known civilizations have state forms of government. The existence of the state thus appears to be a general precondition for the development of civilization. While cities appear to be the most efficient way of organizing the activities of a complex society (and, therefore, there should be a longterm tendency for civilizations to develop cities) at least some early civilizations appear to have lacked them. Moreover, in at least a few instances, cities appear to have existed in the absence of a state. Mecca, down to the time of Mohammed, was an important trading community, yet it lacked a state form of government and the various clans of the Qureish tribe that inhabited it, resorted to blood feuds to settle quarrels among themselves (Wolf 1951). Mecca was clearly not a village, yet authorities argue whether it should be designated a city, or by some less committal term such as town. Similarly, the Yoruba of West Africa have cities, but it is debated whether or not they should be considered as having a civilization. According to our definition, they probably did.

By differentiating these three terms, we are able not only to pinpoint more precisely different aspects of the development of complex societies, but also to see the relationship between disparate theories of social evolution that have been separated more by terminology and historical accident than by logic.

In spite of a good deal of variation in detail, most theories concerning the development of complex societies belong to one of two general types (MacLeod 1924; Lowie 1927).

The first theory sees technological and economic factors as the immediate driving force behind the development of civilization. The unity achieved by such societies is an organic one, promoted by the growing economic interdependence that results from an increasing division of labor. This economic interdependence promotes the development of regional political organizations that facilitate and assure the exchange of goods on a larger scale. This, in turn, promotes increasing social stratification as economic, religious, and military institutions expand and become increasingly hierarchized.

The second type of theory sees political factors as primary among those leading to the development of the state, even though economic motives, such as a desire for land, tribute, or increased sources of labor may underly them. Many such theories postulate that states arise as the result of one group asserting its dominance over another through conquest. The conquerors in such states extract tribute from the conquered and use it to free themselves from the necessity of subsistence production. The term "conquest state," which is frequently applied to states assumed to have originated through coercion, has developed certain unfortunate connotations; in particular, it is associated with the idea that the conquered group is normally ethnically different from the conquerors. Gumplowicz (1963) originally proposed this, arguing that no group of people would be hard-hearted enough to enslave their own tribesmen. The conquest theory is also inadequate because it fails to give recognition to the wide variety of political factors, other than conquest, that can give rise to a state. The nucleus even of many genuine conquest states is an alliance of tribes or villages arrived at through skillful politicing. In any case, the basis of the "politically-derived" state is what Durkheim termed mechanical solidarity, that is, unity achieved either through force or the sharing of similar ideals. This sort of unity can be contrasted with the organic unity achieved by our first type of state through increasing economic interdependence. Michael D. Coe (1961) has called the types of societies that have their origin in these ways *unilateral* and *organic* and these are the terms that we will use for them. It should be understood, however, that both unilateral and organic factors are frequently at work in any particular situation.

The unilateral and organic theories have had rather different scholarly origins. The former were developed by sociologists (Gumplowicz 1963; Oppenheimer 1914) influenced by notions of European history and by ethnologists working mainly in Africa. The organic theory, on the other hand, has been an integral part of prehistorians' speculations about the rise of civilization in the Old and New World. The fact that the former theorists were interested mainly in accounting for the origin of the state, the latter in accounting for the origin of civilization, has meant that the two types of theory were originally formulated with little concern for each other. On the other hand, since the origin of the state and of civilization is clearly interrelated, there has since been a good deal of acrimonious debate between proponents of these two types of theory. Our problem is to understand how much each theory explains and how the two compliment each other.

Most of the older organic explanations of the origin of complex societies were phrased in terms of ecological determinants. The oasis or desiccation hypothesis proposed that a post-Pleistocene decline in rainfall in the Near East destroyed much of the natural vegetation in that area and forced men and animals to live in ever greater proximity to one another around the remaining rivers and oases. This necessitated that men devise more efficient modes of subsistence, through exercising control over the plants and animals about them. Plant and animal domestication led to increases in population and allowed the formation of larger social and economic units, which in turn produced greater social and economic differentiation (Butzer 1964:435–437).

Another monogenic explanation, closely linked to the oasis hypothesis, is the irrigation theory of Karl Wittfogel (1957:13–48; 1959). Wittfogel has seized on one aspect of the oasis theory, namely, that as men were compelled to retreat into the swampy river valleys of the Near East they had to develop systems of flood control and irrigation in order to prosper in this fertile but demanding environment. These hydraulic systems required strong central control to assure their development and maintenance, and this resulted in the growth of a harsh, bureaucratic form of government that Wittfogel calls "Oriental Despotism."

A more elaborate variant of this theory was proposed by Julian Steward (1955:178–209), who argued that as the population of the great river valleys grew, and increasing control over water supplies became necessary, religious sanctions came into play which resulted in the emergence of states that had a theocratic elite. As population pressure continued to grow, the different states began to fight over land and this gradually brought a military class to the fore. Steward (1960) later recognized that trade may be a powerful stimulus to internal differentiation and that a variety of microclimates (small, well-defined areas differing in climate and thus being differentiated in terms of flora and fauna and the crops they are capable of producing) in close proximity to each other may be as much of a stimulus to the development of complex societies as is fertile soil.

The most recent organic theories have tended to avoid seeking a single cause for the origin of complex societies, but instead have concentrated on showing how economic growth in various sectors of the economy can lead to increasing social stratification and the development of the state and of civilization. Robert M. Adams (1960a) has described this process as being linked to the amount of surplus a group produces, the complexity of the subsistence base (as measured by the number of crops grown and the amount of goods exchanged among producers) and finally the intensiveness of land use, only one feature of which is irrigation. This sort of approach, which concentrates on delineating the development of social systems, is exemplified by Adams' (1960b, 1966) description of the development of an organic civilization in Mesopotamia.

Throughout the eighth millennium B.C., food producing economies appear to have developed in the upland regions of Turkey and Persia. After 5500, small agricultural and pastoral communities began to establish themselves in the Tigris and Euphrates river valleys. In this new setting crops became more diversified, small scale irrigation systems developed, and larger surpluses were produced. Arable land (at least near the rivers) grew increasingly valuable and the development of new systems of land ownership encouraged the formation of a stratified society. Disputes over land also tended to drive groups together in defensive and offensive coalitions, while the growing complexity of the subsistence base required new political institutions to integrate the economy. Gradually, a network of urban nuclei began to appear, each serving as a focus for the villages and pastoral communities nearby. It appears that the original centers of economic direction within the cities were the temples, which already in Protoliterate times (3500?–3000 B.C.) were surrounded by a complex of workshops and storerooms. These temples were not only centers of craft specialization, but also redistributive networks embracing large numbers of agricultural dependents. By Early Dynastic times (3000–2425 B.C.), the war leaders of earlier days appear to have become kings. These kings had large landed estates and at first appear to have been concerned mainly with maintaining the city's defenses and raising and outfitting armies. Although local institutions, and the power of secular and temple officials varied from city to city, there was a tendency for secular power to increase, as wars became more common in the Early Dynastic period. The needs of the city states, in turn, stimulated increasing occupation specialization to supply armaments, luxury goods, and mass produced necessities. As a result of these developments, the class structure became increasingly differentiated.

Mesopotamian civilization thus arose in a context of warring city states. The development of occupational specializations, of social stratification, and of economic and political institutions appears to have gone on more or less apace, with developments in one sector of regional life closely linked to those in others. Despite a more or less constant struggle for hegemony among the various city states, no monopoly of power was achieved by any one of them until the Akkadian period (c. 2350 B.C.). Likewise, there was a polycentric distribution of power within each state, and the representatives of various interest groups were sometimes in open conflict with one another. It appears that the city, the various city states, and Mesopotamian civilization as a whole, arose more or less simultaneously and as parts of a single process.

In the development of organic theories, growing attention is now given to ethnographic studies of social and economic development. One of these is Linton's (1933) study of the Tanala of Madagascar. This study shows clearly how social stratification and a strong central government developed in this region as a result of a switch from dry to wet rice cultivation. Prior to the introduction of wet rice, the Tanala were shifting agriculturalists who placed little emphasis on land ownership and had a simple, more or less equalitarian, society. The introduction of wet rice made the relatively small amount of irrigatable land in the valley bottoms especially valuable and not only enhanced the economic and social position of the families that lived there, but also stimulated the development of a strong central government capable of protecting the rights of these new property owners. While other studies have shown that careful schemes to regulate the distribution of land can support a relatively equalitarian society for long periods in spite of such changes (Leach 1961a), Linton's study is nevertheless a valuable illustration of how a state may arise.

Whereas the organic state and organic civilization arise as responses to growing economic complexity, the unilateral state, held together primarily by political factors, can develop under much simpler conditions. The main prerequisites for the latter kind of state are the production of sufficient surpluses to support a ruling class and a relatively sedentary group of producers that will find it difficult to avoid making payments to their rulers. These conditions are found among agriculturalists and among the less mobile cattle pastoralists, but rarely among non food-producing peoples.

In areas where the technology is simple and the means of production are controlled by village cultivators, the chief who aspires to extend his rule must do so by increasing the supply of labor at his command. He can do this by attracting the maximum number of followers, who as farmers and warriors bring in agricultural and craft products in the form of taxes and booty. These can be redistributed by the chief as largess to his supporters and henchmen. The creation of a unilateral state becomes a matter of gaining and holding support in the absence of a division of labor or of resources sufficient enough to promote economic interdependence on a regional level (Fallers 1964).

The problem is how such support is gained. It has been argued that, while conquest is a very effective means of extending power, there are no examples of a stratified society or a state arising from the conquest of one unstratified group by another (MacLeod 1924). The implication of this argument is that all conquest states have developed around a nucleus that was organic to begin with. This argument does not hold, however, simply because all unilateral states are not conquest states.

The nucleus of a state may be formed through alliances based on kinship or ritual ties. The Shilluk kingdom, in the southern Sudan, was based on a common faith in the divinity of the king, combined with a careful manipulation of marriage ties between the royal family and important clans (Gluckman 1965:135–142). Edmund Leach (1954) has described how Kachin chiefs in highland Burma try to set up states in imitation of the Shan lowlanders through the extension of marriage alliances. Normally, however, such states remain loosely knit, like the Shilluk one, or else prove abortive, like the Kachin examples. If, however, they are able to expand through conquest and their rulers can obtain tribute, the power of the latter may increase. The Islamic state is a case in point. This state grew out of a religious movement uniting the bedouin and town dwelling peoples of Arabia. The important centers where the movement developed, Mecca and Medina, were stateless communities prior to Mohammed's time but, the Arab conquest of the ancient civilizations of the Near East quickly transformed the charismaticly-based leadership of the early Islamic state into a powerful secular monarchy.

The nucleus of a unilateral state may be a socially stratified tribal group whose leaders do not possess strong coercive powers. Territorial expansion may transform such a society into a well-organized state. An example is the Zulu Empire. Shaka, born in 1787, distinguished himself as a warrior and invented the stabbing spear and new military tactics which gave the Zulu invincible superiority over their neighbors. In 1818 he became the chief of the Zulu and in a series of ruthless military campaigns extended his influence over a large part of Natal. While his new kingdom was divided into various chiefdoms, the king alone had the right to summon and control the regiments, which were made up of the young men of the kingdom. The king served as a supreme judge and also expelled all rainmakers from the realm, saying that he alone could control the heavens. Gluckman has suggested that an increasing shortage of land and growing trade with the Europeans were two main factors promoting tribal conflict at this time. Shaka was assassinated in 1828 and his successors failed to hold his empire together in the face of internal rivalries and European expansion (Gluckman 1940). Other factors promoting the development of states are the desire of nomadic groups to plunder their sedentary neighbors, of groups driven from their homeland to find a place to live, and of rulers to control trade routes.

The growth of kingdoms through conquest is not confined only to states with a unilateral origin. In Mexico, Mesopotamia, and ancient Greece, states that appear to have developed organically later expanded through conquest and the levying of tribute on their neighbors. At the time of the Spanish conquest, the state of Tenochtitlan was collecting tribute over much of highland Mexico, although it had done little or nothing to interfere with the internal government of the city states that were subject to it. A similar situation appears to have persisted in Mesopotamia until the reign of Sargon, who replaced the governments of the cities he conquered with his own administrators, thereby transforming them into a single (albeit short lived) regional state. The principal characteristic of unilateral states is that they appear to originate along political rather than economic lines, and hence can be constructed on an economic base that is less complex than the one required for the development of organic ones. The tribute paid the leader provides him with the means, not only for attracting and rewarding support to keep him in power, but also for purchasing goods from abroad, supporting a royal court, and attracting skilled artisans to supply his wants. Such a society, if it is large enough and rich enough, can provide a basis for the development of civilization provided that sufficient external stimuli are available. This development normally takes place, however, under the aegis and control of the royal court.

Other differences between organic and unilateral societies can also be noted. Organic ones arise as a result of growing economic interdependence and normally embrace at first only a small region, which has a single city as its nucleus. Such patterns of city states appear to have persisted over long periods in Mesopotamia, highland Mexico, and Greece. Conquest states, on the other hand, can arise quickly and expand to cover vast areas. The Mongol Empire, for example, spread from China to Eastern Europe in one generation. The size of newly developed unilateral states is thus much more variable than that of organic ones. They also differ in stability. Because organic states are a response to economic needs, they have a more stable base, and even if conquered or forced to submit to another state for a long period, may retain their sense of identity. Unilateral states, on the other hand, tend to fall apart very rapidly if the threat of force or the ritual ties that hold them together begin to fail. Because they lack stable nuclei, unilateral states tend to fall apart and replace each other with considerable regularity. Max Gluckman (1965a:143–144) has argued that the main exceptions to this rule are unilateral states which undergo rapid internal differentiation and those which enjoy a large volume of external trade. Both of these factors allow the state to develop an infrastructure approximating the organic type.

In the Old Kingdom, Egypt, unlike Mesopotamia, constituted a single state. At the top of the administrative hierarchy was a king, who was revered as a god and in theory possessed absolute power. From the Fourth Dynasty on, and perhaps even earlier, there was a vizier under the king and under the vizier, various administrative departments, whose power extended down to the local level. At the lowest level in the bureaucratic hierarchy were the village scribes, or headmen, who were responsible for collecting taxes and who handled their community's relations with the district officials. During the Old Kingdom, high ranking officials were transferred from district to district and department to department in the course of their official career. Only as royal power declined, did they begin to remain in a particular place and to accumulate feudal powers there. The taxes, which were paid in kind, were used to support a royal court, the regional administration, and royal works-projects throughout Egypt, as well as to pay for goods imported from abroad, trade in which was a royal monopoly. The most skilled workmen in Egypt were those attached to the court. Officials were rewarded not only with estates but also with gifts from the royal workshops and with tombs built and decorated at royal expense (and originally constructed near the tomb of the reigning monarch). The largest and most enduring monuments of the Old Kingdom are vast pyramid complexes, each made up of the tomb of the reigning Pharaoh, his funerary temples, tombs of the king's relatives and other important officials, the villages of attendant priests, and lands endowed for the support of the complex. The construction of these monuments, which went on generation after generation, must have absorbed a large portion of the revenues of the state and is good evidence of the power and control of the kings at this period (Frankfort 1956:90–120; Adams in Kraeling and Adams 1960:142–143).

Another characteristic of Egyptian civilization, although there is little archeological evidence to go on, is the apparent unimportance of cities prior to the New Kingdom. Although temples were built in various localities, the court appears to have shifted from time to time and there is no evidence of any large urban agglomerations. Much of the specialized production appears to have gone on at the royal court and at government fortresses and estates throughout Egypt, rather than in cities. There are no scenes of urban life in the pictorial representations of the period and the word *niwt,* often translated city, seems to have the more general meaning of settlement. The sprawling town-estates and the dispersed layout of the New Kingdom capital of El Amarna seem to reflect the lack of a strong urban tradition in Egypt.

On purely structural grounds, at least two interpretations of the historical development of the social and political structure of Old Kingdom Egypt are possible. On the one hand, we could infer that Egypt was at a stage of development comparable to Mesopotamia in Sargonid times or later. This would presume that Egypt had originally developed as a series of small city states and that these later had been welded together to form a national state. On the other hand, we could infer that Egypt was a conquest state and that Egyptian civilization had later developed under the aegis of the royal court. From a purely structural point of view either interpretation is possible[2], although the absence of cities, if confirmed, would tend to support the latter. Fortunately, archeological data provides us with the information needed to choose between these two alternatives.

---

[2] For a discussion of the problems involved in inferring historical developments from synchronic structures see Sebag 1964:176–178. There he discusses hypothetical problems involved in reconstructing the history of the U.S. and USSR using only structural data.

6

Predynastic Egypt

IN 1965, Anthony J. Arkell and Peter J. Ucko published a paper entitled *Review of Predynastic Development in the Nile Valley*. In it, they drew attention to serious deficiencies in current knowledge of the prehistoric origins of Egyptian civilization. They attributed most of these deficiencies to "the absence of well-excavated sites." It is true that for various reasons there have been few systematic excavations on prehistoric sites in Egypt in recent years and that most studies have consisted of the reworking of old and rather badly published evidence. No doubt more archeological work, using modern methods, would resolve many problems and would also provide new insights into the nature of the Predynastic period. It is also true, however, (and this point has been dealt with only very tangentially by Arkell and Ucko) that the study of Egyptian prehistory has been further handicapped by a lack of familiarity with methods used by scholars who recently have made great advances in interpreting the development of other early civilizations. It is to this theoretical aspect of the interpretation of the history of Predynastic Egypt that this chapter addresses itself.

The term "Predynastic" embraces all the known food-producing cultures of Egypt prior to the unification of the country around 3000 B.C. The best known sequence has been recovered in Upper Egypt (the part of the country south of modern Cairo) and consists of the Badarian, Amratian, and Gerzean cultures. The continuities between these three cultures are striking and, indeed, it was in attempting to work out a chronology for the graves of the Amratian and Gerzean cultures that Flinders Petrie (1901:4–12) developed his system of Sequence Dating, which employs the basic principles of modern seriation. In an effort to order the graves of these two cultures in temporal sequence, Petrie began to examine fluctuations in the popularity of different types of pottery. Using these as a guide, he worked out a system of 50 successive temporal divisions, which he numbered 30 to 80. The time scale is uncertain, so that we can merely say, for example, that S.D. (SEQUENCE DATE) 49 is earlier than S.D. 50. Also, there is no reason to believe that the amount of time between S.D. 49 and 50 is necessarily the same as that between 60 and 61.

Indeed, the nearer one approaches the historic period the shorter Petrie's divisions appear to be. The importance of the method, from an historical point of view, is that it was based on the assumption of enough continuity in the archeological record to permit the construction of a continuous sequence based on fluctuations in the popularity of various types of artifacts.

Egyptologists were accustomed to beginning the Upper Egyptian sequence with the Tasian culture, which, it was believed, had preceded the Badarian. This culture was defined, however, on the basis of only 30 graves from a single site and the black-incised pottery, which alone distinguished it from the Badarian, is now believed to be intrusive material, probably of Gerzean date. As a result, the Tasian graves are now usually assigned to the Badarian culture (Kantor 1965:4; Arkell and Ucko 1965:150).

Badarian Culture

The Badarian culture, like the other Predynastic ones in Upper Egypt, is known best from cemeteries. These were excavated along the east bank of the Nile in the vicinity of Qau, in Middle Egypt. In addition, Badarian living sites have been found in a layered site at Hammamiya, at Matmar, and Mostagedda, and at the foot of the cliffs in the vicinity of Badari (Baumgartel 1965:7–13; Vandier 1952:191–230). The site at Hammamiya offers stratigraphic evidence that the Badarian culture came to an end before the end of the Amratian. However, the assumption that the Amratian culture developed from the Badarian has been challenged by Werner Kaiser (1956:96–97) who suggests that, since certain types of Amratian pottery are found in some Badarian sites, the two cultures are likely to have been contemporary with each other. Arkell and Ucko (1965:152) have pointed out that the mixture of pottery could have come about through the contamination of an early site with later sherds. Kantor (1965:3–4) has argued even more cogently that it is unlikely these two cultures would have coexisted in the same area and the similarities can better be interpreted as evidence that the Badarian developed into the Amratian.

The remains of the Badarian culture suggest a simple food-producing economy. Bones of cattle, sheep, and goats are listed as found on Badarian sites, although they were not studied by experts to determine whether or not they came from domesticated animals. If the bones of the sheep and goats are correctly identified, they probably were domestic, since no wild species are native to the region; unfortunately, there is the possibility that the bones in question might have been gazelle. These animals were occasionally found wrapped in mats or cloth, and buried like human beings in separate graves in the Badarian cemeteries. This suggests the beginning of a cult of animals, which was to remain strong throughout ancient Egyptian history.

Flint arrowheads, both with a concave base and leaf-shaped, as well as throw sticks, and the bones of fish and birds were present in the sites. Perforated fish-hooks of shell and ivory were found, but harpoon heads are absent. Stone tools were made of nodules of flint gathered along the river, rather than from the tabular flint found in the nearby cliffs. The failure of the Badarians to utilize this better material has been interpreted by some as evidence that they did not originate in this part of the Nile Valley (because they did not know its resources).

Emmer wheat[1] and barley were grown and traces of bread have been found in some graves. Grain was harvested with a wooden sickle, edged with flint, and was stored in clay bins. Castor seeds, probably wild, were collected for their oil. The Badarians wore clothing made of skins with the hair turned inwards and also clothes made of leather and linen. The skins are sometimes interpreted as evidence of a colder climate (Arkell and Ucko 1965:150), although it is well known that the Sumerians, who lived in an even warmer climate, wore sheepskin kilts on some occasions.

Badarian pottery consisted mostly of bowls, usually red in color with a black interior and lip, formed by removing the pot from the kiln red hot and placing it upside down in carbonizing material. Some of these bowls were combed and then burnished before firing. The Badarians also used rectangular slate palettes (presumably for grinding eye paint) and had spoons, vases and figurines made from ivory. Awls and beads were made of cold-hammered copper and there were also beads of steatite covered with blue-green glaze. It has been suggested that these objects were obtained from itinerant travellers coming either from Palestine or across the Red Sea (Arkell and Ucko 1965:150). So little is known about Badarian life, however, that this is far from certain. The evidence could also be used to argue that the Badarian culture was more advanced than is generally believed. The main evidence of trade over long distances consists of shells from the Red Sea and cedar and juniper that is presumed to come from Palestine. Since the climate was more moist then than it is today, it is possible, however, that the wood was indigenous to Egypt.

No evidence of house structures or planning has been noted in any of the Badarian living sites. Presumably the people lived in skin tents or huts made of mats hung on poles. Structures such as these are still used as shelters in Egypt. The site at Mostagedda consisted of a circle of grain pits, outlining an area of ash and pottery.

Cemeteries were located in the desert back of the settlements. The typical Badarian grave was an oval or rectangular pit, roofed with sticks or matting. Graves contained one or more bodies loosely contracted on their left side, with the head south. The body was covered with mats or hides, and pottery and other offerings were placed in the graves. There is no evidence of *sati,* or wife-sacrifice, in the multiple burials, and presumably as long as the roofing remained intact the grave could easily be opened for an additional interment. Neither is there any support for Murray's (1956) claim that until the New Kingdom the common people were buried in the fields or thrown into the river, and that all the graves along the edge of the desert are those of the upper classes. The burials from all periods appear to represent a cross-section of the Egyptian population and the general absence of marked differences in wealth among the graves of the Badarian culture may (but does not necessarily) indicate a lack of social stratification at this time.

---

[1] *Emmer:* a tetraploid species of wheat still grown in Ethiopia.

Amratian Culture

The Amratian or Naqada I culture follows the Badarian and in most respects appears to be derived from it (Baumgartel 1965:13–20; Vandier 1952:230–435 passim). Continuities are seen in the slate palettes, ivory spoons and animal topped combs, as well as in the carving of human and animal figures (Kantor 1965:4). Amratian sites appear to be generally larger and more prosperous than the Badarian ones and are found from Deir Tasa, near Badari in Middle Egypt, as far south as Khor Bahan in Nubia. The most important sites are a large cemetery and two settlements at Naqada and cemeteries near Dendera (Hu) and Abydos (Mahasna and El Amra). The few C¹⁴ dates that are available are between 3800 and 3600 B.C. These dates were obtained soon after the C¹⁴ method was developed and are calculated using the older (and shorter) half life for C¹⁴; moreover, it would appear that because of fluctuations in the rate of C¹⁴ formation, dates for some time prior to 1500 B.C. consistently give C¹⁴ readings that are more recent than their true calendric age (H. S. Smith 1964). As a result, it is probably safer to use C¹⁴ dates from Predynastic Egypt as indications of relative rather than absolute age.

The economy of the Amratian culture appears to have been much the same as that of the Badarian, with agriculture and cattle breeding predominant but hunting and fishing still important. An improvement can be noted in the manufacture of stone tools, most of which were of bifacial construction. The best knives were ground in order to thin them prior to being given their final cutting edge. The most striking of these tools are the fish tail and rhomboidal knives. A few basalt vases with a splayed foot have been found and, since similar vessels are known in Mesopotamia about the same time, there is some question whether these are foreign imports or vessels of local manufacture (Vandier 1952:366–368; Arkell and Ucko 1965:152). Crude stone vessels were manufactured in Badarian times, however (Vandier 1952:216), and these seem to mark the beginnings of a tradition of stoneworking that hereafter was to characterize Egyptian culture; hence, the similarity between the Amratian and Mesopotamian vessels may not prove that the former were of Mesopotamian origin. The ability of the Egyptians to work hard stone during Amratian times is demonstrated by disc shaped maceheads manufactured out of diorite. Crude prototypes for this curious sort of mace are perhaps found in the Badarian culture. Slate palettes were rhomboidal in shape, and later were made in the outline of fish, hippopotami, and antelopes. Copper objects remain small and rare, but now included pins.

Amratian ivory combs have long teeth and are ornamented on the back with naturalistic human and animal figures fashioned in the round. Ivory hippopotamus tusks are carved in the form of (often bearded) human heads. While the black-topped pottery declined in quality and rippling died out early in the Amratian period, red wares remained popular. Some of this pottery was painted with white cross-lined designs and also with scenes showing people and animals, many of the latter in a style typical of Egyptian art in later times. Men are frequently shown wearing feathers in their hair, as the Nubians and Libyans did in historic times, as well as penis sheaths, which were worn until the Early Dynastic period.

A large number of human figurines, both in ivory and in clay, appear to date from this period (Arkell and Ucko 1965:152). Perrot has suggested that the elongated shape of the ankles and face, as well as the drill holes found on the ivory statuettes suggest a cultural affinity with those of the Ghassulian culture, which was flourishing in Palestine about this time (Kantor 1965:7). The exact nature of this cultural connection remains to be demonstrated. Headless bodies and extra skulls found in graves suggest the possibility of headhunting at this time (Murray 1956). It is possible, however, that these finds are related to a more general Amratian custom of dismembering corpses (Vandier 1952:248). As yet I know of no archeological evidence to confirm later traditions of cannibalism in Predynastic times.

A small village of the late Amratian period was excavated at Hammamiya. Nine circular structures, three to seven feet in diameter, were recovered. At least one was a storage room, containing dried dung used for cooking, but another had a hearth near the outer wall and was clearly a small house. The foundations of these buildings were of mud mixed with limestone chips and rough slabs of sandstone. The imprints found on the mud suggest that the superstructures consisted of wattle and daub. It is uncertain whether the settlement near Naqada that Petrie called South Town dates from the Amratian or Gerzean period. In its final stages, this town was fortified and contained quasi-rectangular houses built of mud-brick. In their most .essential features the cemeteries appear little changed from Badarian times.

Gerzean Culture

The Gerzean culture, also called Naqada II, was the culture of Upper Egypt from Amratian times until the unification of the country. In this culture there are signs of more contacts with Southwest Asia, as well as of rapidly increasing population and social stratification.[2] Gerzean sites are found over a greater area than are those of earlier times, extending from the borders of the Delta as far south as the Sudan (Baumgartel 1965:21–32; Vandier 1952:230–435 passim). The main area of cultural activity appears to have been in southern Egypt, in the vicinity of Thebes. Some of the Gerzean towns, such as Hierakonpolis (most of which has never been excavated) appear to have covered a large area and contained rectangular houses built of adobe or mud-brick. A model that was found in a tomb at Diospolis Parva and which appears to show a portion of the wall of a fort or town being guarded by sentinels probably dates from this period (although it might be Amratian). Part of a temple built on a curious elliptical mound has been excavated at Hierakonpolis and this also may date from the Gerzean period (Vandier 1952:518–525). The famous palette of King Narmer was found near this temple.

There are many continuities from Amratian times, particularly in black-topped and polished red vessels and the increasing frequency of Rough Ware. On the other hand, the increasing popularity of light-faced pottery, various fancy

---

[2] It is clear that many cultural changes took place during the Gerzean period and the "culture" should be subdivided into shorter temporal segments if it is to conform with the definition of a culture given in Chapter 3. Kaiser (1957) has already made an effort to do this. The concept of a "Gerzean culture" is retained here merely because it is still in general use.

shaped vessels and a red on buff style of decoration suggest influence from Southwest Asia. Baumgartel has argued that there is a genetic link between various motifs used in this latter style of decoration and ones found in Iran. Scharff, Frankfort, and others deny this. After a careful survey of conflicting points of view, Vandier (1952:356–363) has concluded:

> The influence one sees has not been very profound. It concerns rather an inspiration or better still a point of departure that the Gerzeans may have borrowed from their neighbours to the east. Perhaps it is even necessary to renounce a point of departure and to admit that the motifs common to these cultures were created independently in the two countries. The very simplicity of the designs suggests such an hypothesis (p. 363).

The slow potter's wheel was introduced during Gerzean times and was used to turn out tops of narrow-mouthed vessels. It is also likely that many types of pottery, previously manufactured on a small scale in villages throughout Upper Egypt, were now produced in vast numbers in a few centers.

During the Gerzean period flint tools were manufactured by a technique of controlled ripple flaking. The finest products of this technique are some thin swordlike knives and those of the older fish-tailed design. Near the start of the Gerzean phase the flat-topped mace[3] was replaced by a pear-shaped variety resembling those used in Mesopotamia. This form appears to have diffused to Upper Egypt from the Delta, where it probably was known in Amratian times. Copper tools, such as celts, daggers, harpoons, knives, needles, and rings were now being cast and apparently were manufactured in some abundance.

There is also a great improvement in native arts and crafts. Decoration is more finely conceived and formally arranged than ever before and the execution of designs is frequently of high quality. Although the crude thirteen foot high statues of the god Min that were found at Coptos are no longer believed to date from the Predynastic period, at least one smaller statue has been found that is carved in basalt and represents a god or a bearded worshipper. Zoomorphic vessels were made in hard stone and took such varied forms as elephants, birds, fish, and tortoises (Vandier 1952:306–317). Beads and amulets increase in number and quality and are produced in exotic stones such as lapis lazuli as well as in gold and silver. These objects suggest not only technological advances but also the development of an elite interested in having luxury goods.

New building materials and greater formality in art and architecture are indications of the cultural changes that characterize this period. Evidence of social stratification can be found in the growing diversity in size and design of tombs. Many of the more elaborate ones are lined with planks and have several chambers, and at Hierakonpolis a so-called "royal tomb" has been found that dates from late Gerzean times. The walls of this tomb were plastered and covered with paintings in which motifs of Egyptian and Asian origin are found side by side. A similar melange of local and foreign motifs is found on the ivory handle of the Gebel el Arak knife (p. 83), which was not found in situ but appears to date from this period.

---

[3] *Mace:* a heavy club.

This blending of local and foreign motifs is further evidence that traits of Asian origin were reaching Egypt at this time.

The culture of the period around 3000 B.C. that saw the unification of Egypt used to be called the Semainian. Today, however, this term has been dropped and the unification of Egypt is used to mark the dividing line between the Gerzean and Early Dynastic periods. The use of political criteria to define cultural phases is not entirely satisfactory, however, and it would still be useful to have a name such as Semainian to denote the period of intense cultural activity that marked late Gerzean times and the first few decades of the First Dynasty. This period saw the initial development of Egyptian writing and of a monumental style of panelled brick architecture. Copper tools and vessels became more common and the artistic accomplishments of the period are exemplified in dishes made of schist[4] and alabaster as well as by royal palettes, tomb stelae, and the beginnings of monumental sculpture. During the same period, the beautifully decorated pottery of Predynastic times gave way to simpler, more utilitarian varieties. Evidence of increasing social stratification and growing royal power is seen soon after the unification of Egypt in the sacrifice and burial of retainers in the royal tombs. In spite of these novel developments, the best evidence of underlying cultural continuity is that Petrie's Sequence Dates are now known to continue well into the Early Dynastic period, the unification having taken place around s.d. 65.

Lower Egypt

The Predynastic cultures of Lower Egypt (that is, the Delta) are not as well known as those in the south and comparability between the two regions is reduced because the cultures in the north are known mainly through settlements, those in the south through cemeteries. The main sites found so far are located at the apex of the Delta and along its edges, and these suggest that in Predynastic times the cultural traditions of this region were different from those to the south. The individual sites are considerable distances apart and so far it has been impossible to construct a cultural sequence comparable to the one for Upper Egypt. It is believed that few Predynastic sites may ever be found in the Delta proper, since most appear to be concealed under more recent deposits of alluvium.

The Fayum A culture, found southwest of Cairo, is C^{14} dated around 4400 B.C. (Vandier 1952:65–94; Hayes 1965:93–99). The sites belonging to this culture were excavated along the north and northeast banks of an ancient lake, that apparently was in the process of declining. The excavation reports suggest (again without confirmation by a specialist) that the bones of domestic sheep and goats (and perhaps cattle, although there probably were wild cattle in the vicinity) may have been present and two groups of underground granaries were excavated containing emmer wheat and barley. No house structures were found and the encampments probably consisted of reed or mat huts placed in the lee of buttes or mounds close to fertile strips of soil by the edge of the lake. The granaries were located in

---

[4] *Schist:* a crystalline rock that can be split easily into layers.

areas of high ground adjoining, but not inside, the settlements. Large animals were hunted, including elephant and hippopotamus, and fish and mussels were taken from the lake. Small harpoons and bevelled points made of bone were found, but no fishhooks. The harpoons are said to resemble those from Palestine, rather than the kind found farther south in the Sudan and in East Africa. Shell ornaments appear to have come from both the Mediterranean and the Red Sea. The arrowheads resemble those found in the Badarian culture and also the Aterian culture farther west. There were sickle flints set in wooden handles and stone gouges with polished cutting edges. Aside from the latter, the shape of which is functionally determined to a large degree and the same in cultures in many parts of the world, there is nothing about the Fayum A culture that would suggest any affinities with the Khartoum culture in the south (Arkell 1961:33, 34). The presence of amazonite beads in both cultures does not prove they were both in contact with a common source, since this stone is found in the deserts east of the Nile Valley as well as in the Tibesti mountains to the west, where Arkell argues it must have come from.

Baskets were common, and were used to line the granaries, and rough linen cloth was also manufactured. The pottery was made from coarse clay and consisted of bag-shaped vessels and flat bottomed dishes, some with a burnished red slip, others with a plain rough surface. No incised, combed, or painted pottery was found. McBurney (1960:233–238) suggests that this pottery, as well as the sickles, show connections with the coastal areas of the Levant.

One problem with Fayum A is that of correlating it with other cultures in Egypt. C[14] dates suggest that it may be the earliest food-producing culture known in the Nile Valley and there are many general parallels between it and the Badarian culture. Unfortunately, no comparable C[14] dates are available for Badarian; nor do we have any idea how early the latter culture began. The main basis for arguing that Fayum A is earlier than Badarian is the total absence of metal in Fayum A. Metal is also lacking at Merimde, however, a site which is probably contemporary with the Amratian culture. This suggests that the use of metal may have begun in Upper Egypt earlier than in the north and that perhaps metal working developed in the Nile Valley independently of its development in Southwest Asia.[5]

The large stratified site of Merimde, is located on the western edge of the Delta (Vandier 1952:95–153; Hayes 1965:103–116). It covers an area of 215,000 square yards and the cultural debris has an average depth of seven feet. The C[14] dates for the uppermost layer of this site are about 3530 B.C.; for the lowest about 600 years earlier. The pottery and the stone celts, sickles, and arrowheads tend to resemble those of Fayum A. Some of the red pottery is decorated with patterns of contrasting smooth and rough finish and black-topped pottery has been found at Merimde as well. Polished black pottery is found only in the upper layers of the site. The houses and shelters in the topmost level are oval, semisubterranean structures, their lower portions built of clods of mud, probably covered over on the top with a wattle and daub superstructure, like the huts found at Hammamiya. A considerable number of burials was made inside the village, a custom found also in Palestine, but not in Upper Egypt. The pear-shaped maces found at Merimde appear

---

[5] Copper used to be believed to come from the Sinai Peninsula. Now it appears likely that sources also existed in southern Egypt.

to be derived from Asian models and to be the prototypes of the Gerzean ones. Kantor (1965:5) is of the opinion that the round houses, the carinated bowls and a special sort of vessel supported by four modelled human feet put Merimde in the general time range of the Amratian culture. This is supported by the C^{14} dates.

Another site, rather similar to Merimde is that of El Omari, located just south of Cairo (Vandier 1952:154–166; Hayes 1965:116–122). The pottery and stone tools from the two sites are much alike, although the vases from El Omari are larger and lack handles. As at Merimde, the houses are round and burials were made inside the village. On typological grounds, Junker was of the opinion that El Omari was earlier than Merimde. Today, although stratigraphic evidence is lacking, it is generally believed to be later. This conclusion is supported by a single C^{14} date of 3306 B.C. Most of the bodies found at El Omari face west with the head pointed south, a custom that suggests Upper Egyptian influence. One skeleton, thought to be that of a local chief, was found holding a wooden staff fourteen inches long. This suggested to Childe what Hayes has correctly described as "the rather far-fetched notion" that one of the Omari chieftains might have become the King of Lower Egypt.

Maadi is a still later site near Cairo (Vandier 1952:466–496; Hayes 1965:122–134). The many objects of Upper Egyptian provenience found there show that it is almost certainly of Gerzean date. Maadi is a sprawling town of oval huts, rectangular houses, and cave-like subterranean chambers that were used as magazines. There is evidence that copper ore was imported and worked there in considerable quantities. Probably it came from the Sinai peninsula. The local pottery is similar in many ways to that of the Gerzean culture and this, along with other features, suggests the increasing influence of the south already noted at El Omari. Maadi also has yielded a large amount of pottery, whose composition, as well as the shape, suggests that it came from Palestine in Early Bronze Age I times. This also helps to assure a Gerzean date for the site.

In spite of the work done at these sites, the cultures of Lower Egypt are still poorly defined. They are distinguished from those of Upper Egypt by their monochromate, often undecorated, pottery and by a general scarcity of jewelry, sculpture, and decoration. Pigs, either tame or wild, seem to have been more popular in Lower Egypt than in the south and various ritual practices, such as the burial of individuals within the settlement, seem restricted to this region. It has been suggested that the surviving settlements in Lower Egypt are considerably larger than those farther south and that this may indicate a greater emphasis on incipient urban life in this region. This may equally well be an accident of preservation or of recovery, however.

The Validity of the Evidence

The archeology of Predynastic Egypt suggests a course of development different from that of Southwest Asia. In the latter, a series of food-producing cultures has been found that goes as far back as 8000 B.C. In the highlands of Turkey and in the Levant, large settlements such as Jericho, Chatal Huyuk, and Hacilar were flourishing before the seventh millennium and the beginnings of metallurgy are noted as early as 5000 B.C. Settlement appears to have begun on the plains of Mesopotamia soon afterwards. There, as the Protoliterate culture took shape during the fourth millennium, villages grew into cities, and writing was invented. In Egypt, the Neolithic or food-producing period appears to have started later and civilization appears to have developed faster.

Such, at least, is the accepted interpretation of the archeological record. Arkell and Ucko (1965:155), however, have quite properly questioned whether the food-producing period actually began in Egypt as late as prehistorians believe, or if the archeological record is not in some way incomplete or wrongly interpreted.[6] This raises a set of difficult problems concerning the adequacy both of the current data and of the models we use to interpret them. Some of these problems could be treated separately if we could be sure that the Badarian culture actually was as primitive as it is presumed to be. If it were, the development of civilization in Upper Egypt would have been a rapid process no matter how long a rudimentary food producing economy had existed in the area. Unfortunately, this is not certain since the rudimentary metal goods and glazed beads found in Badarian sites may actually be of local manufacture and be an indication of other things we do not know about the Badarian culture. The development of a more complex technology and corresponding social changes may have begun in Upper Egypt prior to Gerzean or even Amratian times.

Any attempt to assess the present state of knowledge concerning Predynastic Egypt requires an evaluation of both the archeological evidence and all the evidence from related fields that either provides us with independent information concerning Egyptian history or else influences our interpretation of archeological findings. The point has recently been made that social anthropologists err when they attempt to evaluate and make use of data outside their field of professional competence (Gluckman 1964). Whatever value the limiting of one's theoretical perspectives may have for social anthropologists, this is advice that cannot be heeded by the prehistorian, who must be prepared to compare and to utilize data from many different fields in order to reconstruct a picture of the past. This does not mean, of course, that such information should be used in a cavalier fashion, or that Gluckman's caveats to social anthropologists do not apply to prehistorians as well. What it does mean is that prehistorians cannot narrow their theoretical perspectives, but rather must cope with the problems of using findings from fields that lie outside their own sphere of competence.

---

[6] The importance of this question is underlined by the fact that as this book was going to press a report was circulating that Fred Wendorf believes he has found traces of late Paleolithic hunters and fishers living in a savanna environment in Nubia around 12,500 B.C. The use of grasses by these people is attested by the presence of sickles and grinding stones. Whether they cultivated cereals or harvested wild seeds is not yet determined. The only reference in writing to this find I have come across is in a footnote in the *American Scientist* 55 (1967), p. 342. Students should be alert for future discussions of this find.

It should also be noted that domestic sheep or goats were present at the site of Haua Fteah, in Cyrenaica, by 6000 B.C. The presence of animals of Asian origin this far west suggests that they had already been introduced into at least northern Egypt by this time.

Geological Evidence

One of the most important fields related to the interpretation of Egyptian prehistory is Pleistocene geology. The findings of geologists are important for evaluating a number of opposing views concerning the original nature of the Nile Valley and the climate of the region, each of which could influence differently our understanding of the course of Egyptian history in Predynastic times.

Many Egyptologists have been impressed by Herodotus' claim that Egypt was an arm of the sea which became filled with silt deposited by the Nile, as well as by the frequent depiction of marshes in Egyptian tombs and Egyptian stories of how the world was created on a sand hill rising out of the primeval waters. They have believed that these stories preserve memories of a time when the valley was a vast swampland, unsuited for permanent settlement. At first, human beings lived only along the edges of the valley, locating their campsites at the foot of the cliffs or on top of rocky promontories. Only as the highlands turned into deserts was man forced to settle in this jungle-like environment and to begin the long and arduous process of clearing it. Both Siegfried Passarge (1940) and Karl W. Butzer (1959) have studied this problem from a geographic point of view and have come to the conclusion that the topography of the valley is such that swamps were always a minor feature of the landscape, except in the northern Delta. Most of the plain consisted of seasonally flooded natural basins which supported grasses and brush vegetation during the dry season. The higher levees along the river were covered with trees, such as acacia, tamarisk, and sycamore, and ones that remained permanently out of the water were available for year-round habitation. The idea that men were forced to settle in the Nile Valley by deteriorating conditions on the adjacent steppes, is vitiated by evidence that the Neolithic period in Egypt corresponded to a period of increased rainfall in North Africa. During this period, usually called the "Neolithic Wet Phase" the Sahara became for a time far more habitable than it is today.[7]

While Passarge's and Butzer's view is generally accepted as far as the Nile Valley south of Cairo is concerned, there is still considerable debate concerning the nature of the Delta. It was once believed that the Delta had rapidly extended seaward in historic times as a result of the continued deposition of alluvium by the river. More recently, the geologist Rhodes Fairbridge (Arkell and Ucko 1965:159) has suggested that small changes in sea level periodically have forced the population from low lying regions of the Delta. Butzer (1959), on the other hand, argues that the Delta has not extended seaward in historic times and that physical conditions in this area in Predynastic times were little different from what they are today.

Speculations about the Delta have played an important role in arguments concerning the relative cultural importance of Upper and Lower Egypt in Predynastic times. Some authorities have suggested that large areas of high ground in the

---

[7] For a healthy, but still inconclusive, challenge to the theory of substantial long-term oscillations in the climate in post-Pleistocene times see Robert Raikes, *Water, Weather and Prehistory*. London: John Baker, 1967.

southern Delta were dotted with farming villages similar to those "of the Fayum and of the adjoining areas of southwestern Asia" (Hayes 1965:103). Others have suggested that the Egyptians living in the Delta were a sedentary farming people living in thickly clustered villages, whereas the Upper Egyptians were "mainly a nomadic folk" (Edwards 1964:34). Hermann Junker even proposed that burial inside the settlement, such as was found at Merimde and El Omari, was an earmark of settled life, whereas burial away from the settlement, as practiced in Upper Egypt was a trait of nomadic peoples (Hayes 1965:112). The latter suggestion is, of course, ethnographically unsound. Still other Egyptologists have argued that Egyptian civilization developed in Lower Egypt and spread from there south. The principal supports for these arguments are the greater proximity of the Delta to Southwest Asia, the greater richness of the soil (already noted by Herodotus, who described the Delta as the easiest land to work in the world) and various Egyptian myths, which, it is claimed, indicate that the first Egyptian kingdom evolved in Lower Egypt.

Opponents of this brand of theory have looked to claims that the Delta was either under water or else too swampy to be habitable as an easy way to demolish it. If conditions of this sort prevailed over most of the Delta, then the cultures in northern Egypt would have been peripheral and unimportant. Baumgartel, for example, has argued that the Delta was unfit for human habitation much before the Dynastic period. Scholars on both sides have usually been content to quote the geological claims that happen to fit their own preconceptions of Egyptian prehistory, without attempting to assess the various arguments in an objective sort of way. Yet it is clear that a sound approach to these problems requires the prehistorian to examine rival claims carefully in order to judge their merits for himself. In my opinion, Butzer's conclusions concerning the Delta, which are based on the study of soil samples obtained from bore holes, are more convincing than those of Fairbridge, which are based on a hypothetical reconstruction of worldwide climate and sea levels. Geology thus appears to be no *deus ex machina* resolving the problem of the cultural relationships between Upper and Lower Egypt in Predynastic times.

Another problem that bears examination from a geological point of view is the lack of reported sites between Upper Paleolithic times and the Fayum A and Badarian cultures. Only a few camp sites have been found that date from this period and those from Helwan, near Cairo, contain various stone tools that are said to have affinities with the Natufian culture in Palestine. We must enquire, therefore, if the explanation for this apparent gap is some sort of archeological shortcoming, such as a former lack of interest in sites that do not contain pottery, or whether some geological reason makes sites from this period especially hard to find.

It appears that throughout history most settlements have been built on the floodplain, while in Upper Egypt at least cemeteries have frequently been located in the desert just beyond the edge of the cultivation. As a result, most living sites, except those located on high ground or built, like the town of Kom Ombo, on *tells* formed by the debris of earlier villages, have long ago either been buried under more recent deposits of silt or have been washed away by changes in the course of the river. This explains the low ratio of Predynastic living sites to cemeteries that has been recovered in Upper Egypt. Butzer (1960) also suggests that between 8000 and 5000 B.C. the Nile floods were lower than they are today and the valley narrower. Hence, even the cemeteries that were located along the margin of the flooded land at that time are now buried under more recent deposits of alluvium. Similarly, it has been shown that many Predynastic sites in Middle Egypt (hitherto often considered uninhabited in Predynastic times) either have been destroyed by shifts in the channel of the river or else have been buried under later deposits. This suggests that the known distributions of sites from different periods may not be historically as significant as they appear to be. The Badarian culture, for example, may have been present throughout much of Upper Egypt and the Amratian culture may have extended almost as far north as the Gerzean. The richest and culturally most advanced communities in Upper Egypt were probably built on now-buried levees along the banks of the river, and thus remain unknown to us.

Language

A second area in which important debates concerning problems of the history of Predynastic Egypt continue to be waged is that of language. The numerous similarities in grammar, lexicon,[8] and phonology[9] between ancient Egyptian and the Semitic languages have long been apparent and it has been argued that Egyptian is either a Semitic language obscured by change or else a creole language[10] resulting from the mixing, in Predynastic times, of an "African" and a Semitic language. This African language is sometimes identified as Hamitic (which sometimes is, and sometimes is not, believed to be distantly related to Semitic) and sometimes as a "Negro language" (Lambdin 1961:289–290). This theory of creolization has, of course, stemmed from, and in turn been used to support, the theory that there were various migrations into Egypt from Southwest Asia in prehistoric times and that these have resulted in ethnic and cultural changes.

Egyptian borrowings from Semitic languages are well attested in historic times, and Kees and others are no doubt well-founded in their conclusion that the Semitic languages exerted a strong influence over Egyptian in the late Predynastic period (corresponding with the archeological evidence of strong West Asian influences in the realm of art and material culture). There is, however, no evidence of an "African substratum" in ancient Egyptian, in the sense that it can be demonstrated that all of the similarities with the Semitic languages found in Egyptian are borrowings superimposed on an identifiable, and presumably indigenous, African language. On the contrary, Greenberg (1955:43–61) has shown that while there definitely are Semitic borrowings in ancient Egyptian, many of the similarities between these languages are genetic in origin and indicate that both are derived from a common ancestor. Greenberg argues that Semitic and ancient Egyptian, plus the other three language groups located in North Africa—Kushitic, found in Abyssinia

[8] *Lexicon:* the total stock of morphemes or the vocabulary of a language.
[9] *Phonology:* the system of speech sounds of a language.
[10] *Creolization:* the formation of a mixed language that develops when speakers of mutually unintelligible languages remain in long-standing and intimate contact with each other.

and to the east of the Nile, and Berber and Chadic found in the western Sahara—form five coordinate branches of an Afroasiatic[11] language family. The basic similarities among all the languages belonging to this family result from their origin in the same speech community. Greenberg (personal communication) has a general impression that Old Kingdom Egyptian and Akkadian, (a roughly contemporary Semitic language) appear to be a bit further apart than Rumanian and Portuguese are today, which suggests the period between 5500 and 6000 B.C. as the time for the original separation of the Afroasiatic languages. Chadic and Berber may have spread into the western Sahara during the Neolithic Wet Phase that followed. It has been suggested that the variations among the Kushitic languages favor the eastern Sudan as a place of origin for this language family (Lewis, n.d.), but, since two main branches of the Afroasiatic family are found on either side of the Nile Valley, Egypt itself is a possible candidate.

In any case, it appears quite likely that the Predynastic cultures of Upper (and Lower) Egypt were associated with a people who already spoke Egyptian and that later Semitic borrowings came from a closely related group of languages. Since many of the similarities between Egyptian and Semitic are due to common origin, these borrowings are much less spectacular than was believed, and certainly they cannot be safely construed as evidence of creolization or massive population mergers. Of the hypothesized non-Afroasiatic "African substratum," no trace exists.

Oral Traditions

A third source of historical information has been sought in the field of Egyptian mythology. The German Egyptologist, Kurt Sethe, interpreted certain Egyptian myths concerning a struggle between the gods Horus and Seth as a reflection of the conquest of Upper Egypt by Lower Egypt in prehistoric times. This conquest was assumed to have been carried out by Osiris, who later became the god of the Delta town of Busiris. Later, an Upper Egyptian rebellion under the banner of Seth was crushed by the Lower Egyptians, under Horus, the chief god of the Western Delta, and a second northern kingdom was founded with its capital at Heliopolis (Griffiths 1960:145–146). This historical interpretation of the Horus and Osiris myths gave rise to much speculation concerning the culture of this prehistoric northern kingdom. Eduard Meyer attributed to it the invention of the Egyptian calendar, based on the heliacal rising of Sirius, in 4236 B.C. (Kees 1961:43). This calendar is now generally believed to have been invented one cycle later, about the start of the Third Dynasty. It has also been argued that Sethe's theory is supported by the Palermo Stone, a year by year record of the Egyptian kings that was compiled in the Fifth Dynasty. Here some Predynastic kings are pictured wearing the Red Crown of the Delta and perhaps the united crowns of Upper and Lower Egypt.

[11] *Semitic/Hamitic:* Semitic is a linguistic term referring to a group of historically related languages found in early historic times in Southwest Asia. Arabic and Hebrew are modern languages belonging to this family. The term Hamitic has been applied to various languages in North Africa that show a more distant relationship to Semitic. Greenberg has proposed a more refined classification according to which Kushitic, ancient Egyptian, Berber, Chadic, and Semitic are seen as five equal branches from an original Afroasiatic language.

Only the names of these kings are recorded, which appears to indicate that no information was available in the Fifth Dynasty concerning their activities. It has been suggested that these figures represent mythical demigods, believed to have ruled Egypt between the time of the gods and the first human kings. Such beings were required by Egyptian conceptions of history and cosmogony and their names may have no historical significance whatsoever.

Not one, but many differing historical interpretations have been applied to these myths. Kees and Siegfried Schott have argued that since Horus and Seth both are attested in Upper Egypt in Predynastic times, their fight refers to a political crisis in Upper Egypt which preceded the conquest of the north. Baumgartel has even suggested that the story refers to the conquest of the "Amratian town" of Nubet, sacred to the god Seth, by the "Gerzean people," whose kings were worshippers of Horus (Griffiths 1960:131–134). It has also been suggested that the struggle took place in the Second Dynasty, when a line of kings bearing traditional Horus names was interrupted by a king who assumed a name in honor of the god Seth (Griffiths: 138–139). It is not unworthy to point out in connection with the latter suggestion that even more or less historical events remain exceedingly obscure.

Other scholars, notably Henri Frankfort (1948:15–23), have rejected an historical interpretation for these myths. Frankfort argues that both the idea of a Double Kingdom of Upper and Lower Egypt and the myth of the struggle of Horus and Seth reflect an Egyptian pattern of thought that sees totality comprised of opposites in balanced opposition. When they described Egypt as two kingdoms, the early rulers were attempting to provide religious sanctions for their government by establishing a congruency between it and the cosmological conceptions of the Egyptian people. By identifying the king with Horus and Seth, perennial symbols of strife, they were merely formulating a mythical charter for the monarch's role as the king of the whole of Egypt.

If Frankfort's interpretation is correct, the idea of a Northern Kingdom could have been created as a counterpart to the southern one after, rather than before, the conquest of the whole country. In Predynastic times Egypt may have consisted, not just of two, but of a series of small states, which the Early Dynastic kings conquered piecemeal. As we know, little archeological evidence has been found that can shed light on political conditions in the Delta in Predynastic times. The discovery of a representation of the Red Crown of Lower Egypt on a piece of Amratian pottery from Upper Egypt has been used to argue that a kingdom of Lower Egypt did exist in Predynastic times although the extent of the kingdom is in doubt. It is possible, however, that prior to dynastic times this crown was a symbol of the goddess Neith rather than of kingship. Kees, who believes that several different ethnic groups may have lived in the Delta, has suggested that, since only the northwestern part of the Delta appears to have been ethnically different from Upper Egypt (he believes that the representations on Upper Egyptian palettes from late Predynastic times suggest a strong Libyan component in this region), it alone may be referred to when the Egyptians speak of the conquest of Lower Egypt.

It is clear that, whatever the origins of these ancient Egyptian myths really were, they can only be interpreted in the light of what we already know about the historical events of the time and about the myth making processes of the ancient

Egyptians. They cannot be used by themselves as a basis for inferring historical events. It is clear that much of the ritual of ancient Egypt had its origin in Predynastic times. The development of the mortuary complex and possibly the veneration of animals can be traced back to the Badarian culture and various historic deities, or their symbols, seem to be already present in the Amratian culture. The systematic study of this evidence may eventually shed some light on the nature of Egyptian religion in Predynastic times and this may allow us to assess with more precision the ideological background of these myths. Further archeological evidence may allow us to understand better their historical background. Until more such evidence is available, however, the use of these myths for historical purposes can only serve to confuse the main issues.

Physical Anthropology

A fourth source of auxiliary information is Physical Anthropology. Just as some philologists try to see an "African substratum" in the Egyptian language, so some physical anthropologists try to demonstrate that the earliest Predynastic population of Egypt was Negroid, and see, in any Caucasoid element, evidence of the later migration of Hamito-Semitic types into the country. Too often, there has been a tendency to attribute the cultural development of Egypt to the repeated incursions of people of the latter type. Batrawi (1945–1946), on the other hand, has shown through a careful study of the skeletal evidence that there was very little change in physical type in Upper Egypt through Predynastic or Dynastic times. Although there was some variation within the population, the Upper Egyptian people were mostly small in stature and had long narrow skulls, dark wavy hair, and brown skin. This continuity in physical type does not provide evidence of migration or gene flow, although it does not rule out the possibility that new groups of a similar physical type entered the country from time to time.

The most recent employment of physical anthropological evidence to argue a migration has been Emery's (1961:39–40) acceptance of D. E. Derry's theory of a "Dynastic Race" as proof that the Early Dynastic civilization was brought into Egypt by a "civilized aristocracy or master race" that Emery claims possibly originated along the Indian Ocean and also laid the foundations of Sumerian civilization. I. E. S. Edwards (1964:35–36) has suggested, somewhat more cautiously, that at least the "fresh knowledge they brought with them" accounts for the "acceleration in cultural progress observable at this time." According to Derry's (1956) analysis, a race of massively built, mesocephalic people entered Egypt about the start of the First Dynasty. He suggested that they came from Asia and could be identified with the Armenoid physical type found in that region. By the end of the First Dynasty, they had penetrated as far south as Abydos and gradually were merging with the indigenous population.

This evidence must be treated with great caution. The population of the Delta has always maintained contacts with Southwest Asia and its people consequently have tended to resemble those to the east more than have the people of Upper Egypt. The skeletons found at Merimde, El Omari and Maadi suggest that the Predynastic inhabitants of the Delta were taller and more sturdily built than the people of Upper Egypt, and that their skulls were broader (Hayes 1965:135). These people appear similar, and probably were ancestral, to Derry's "Dynastic Race." They also suggest that individuals of the Armenoid type, common in Syria and Lebanon, were entering the Delta and interbreeding with the local population far earlier than the start of the First Dynasty. So far, no evidence has been found of the intrusive sites or migration routes needed to prove that any large-scale migration of these people entered Egypt at any time during the Predynastic period. Until such evidence is forthcoming, it is better to assume that whatever gene flow went on in late Predynastic times was incidental to cultural development. To go further and attribute the Early Dynastic culture, or any earlier one, to the appearance of a "master race" is to transgress all permissible limits of scientific inference.

Migrations and Diffusion

Most early interpretations of cultural development in Predynastic Egypt were based on two very closely related premises: (1) that culture change came about as the result of the appearance of new peoples who blended with the local population and contributed traits from their own culture to the existing one, and (2) that advances in culture were the result of the conquest of culturally (and often racially) inferior people by groups that were more advanced.

Although Lower Egypt has played an important part in speculations about the development of Egypt as a whole, the scarcity of evidence has tended to restrict speculation concerning the significance of the cultures of this region. Connections with various neighboring regions have been noted. Arrowheads and stonework are similar to those found in the western Sahara and the animals, pottery, sickles, and harpoons seem to be of Southwest Asian origin. Except, however, for the trade goods from Maadi, most of these proposed cultural connections are still rather tenuous. Similarities with Upper Egypt are frequent, even in earliest times, and Upper Egyptian influence grows stronger as the historic period is approached. Arkell and Baumgartel have proposed a number of connections with the Sudan, but these are very general ones and consequently are highly uncertain (Hayes 1965:135–136). In spite of these far-flung connections, the distinctively local character of Lower Egyptian culture is generally recognized.

There is also the question how much the differences in material culture between Upper and Lower Egypt are indicative of differences in other spheres of culture. Cyril Aldred (1965:41) has argued that it is wrong to exaggerate the cultural differences between the two regions. Both appear to have shared the same language and had many of the same religious beliefs in Predynastic times, and this underlying unity of thought and feeling explains why the whole country was able to develop so quickly once it was united. The strong cultural influence that Upper Egypt wielded over the whole country from Gerzean times onward suggests that the Delta was culturally, as well as politically, weaker than the south and Kees (1961:33–34) has argued that even in historic times it was regarded as an area of colonization. The known sites, however, all are in marginal areas and culturally more advanced ones may have existed inside the Delta, on the site of historic towns such as Tanis, Bubastis, and Mendes. To what degree certain historic forms of architecture and rituals that are believed to be of Lower Egyptian origin really are, and how much the culture of Lower Egypt contributed to the mainstream of Egyptian cultural development must remain a matter for speculation. Fortunately, since the unification of Egypt was brought about by a king from Upper Egypt and the national culture of Early Dynastic times appears to be largely a continuation and development of the Gerzean one, the Upper Egyptian sequence can, in most respects, be treated as representing the prehistoric foundations of Egyptian culture.

In a synthesis written in 1939, Flinders Petrie presented an outline of Egyptian prehistory in which the migration model was carried to a heady extreme. According to Petrie, the Fayum culture represented a "Solutrean migration from the Caucasus," which was also the homeland of the Badarian people. The Amratian White-lined pottery was introduced by "Libyan invasions," whereas the Gerzean culture was brought in by the "Eastern Desert Folk" who invaded and dominated Egypt. Finally, Egypt was unified by the "Falcon Tribe" or "Dynastic Race" which "certainly had originated in Elam" (in Persia) and came to Egypt by way of Ethiopia and the Red Sea. In each case, Petrie's arguments were based on a rather tenuous connection between a few traits in the Egyptian culture being discussed and those in some culture outside of Egypt, while the culture pattern as a whole was ignored. The Fayum and Badarian cultures were linked with the Solutrean (which is a western European culture, unknown in the Caucasus) on the basis of certain general similarities in their traditions of stone-working. Petrie was unabashed by the fact that over 10,000 years separated the last manifestations of the Solutrean culture from the Egyptian ones he was discussing. Since virtually nothing was known of Libyan archeology his conclusions about the origin of the Amratian vessels were purely gratuitous and his evidence concerning the Gerzean culture and the "Dynastic Race" was likewise extremely tenuous.

At first glance, Petrie's conclusions are unexpected, since all of the principles of Sequence Dating developed and applied by him to the Amratian and Gerzean cultures, rest on an assumption of cultural continuity, which allows for only gradual stylistic changes. Moreover, the results of his pottery seriation had demonstrated clearly the many continuities in shape, design, fabric, and decorative motifs, that linked these periods together. There was no evidence whatsoever of clear breaks between the Predynastic cultures of Upper Egypt, nor did the innovations found at the start of one culture exceed the numerous continuities that linked it with the one preceding. If Petrie had not been thinking in terms of a model that assumed cultural changes to be brought about by changes in population, he would have had no trouble explaining the cultural development of Upper Egypt in Predynastic times as a single ongoing process, with those traits that are, or are suspected of being, of foreign origin finding their place within a well-established, but dynamic, continuum. Only because he was thinking in terms of the most fasionable model of the day, which attributed all culture change to the movement of peoples, did he interpret the traits carried over from one period to the next as resulting from the survival of an indigenous population, and new traits as the result of ideas new groups brought with them when they came to blend with, or rule over, these people.

In each case, he probably assumed that the blending of the two groups took place quickly, so that the incoming group left behind no traces of its independent existence.

This particular approach to Egyptian prehistory (although not the details of Petrie's account) has remained influential until the present. Its main opponents have been Henri Frankfort and Helene Kantor, who both have stressed continuities rather than discontinuities in Egyptian prehistory. We will outline some of the current migrationary theories, period by period, and attempt to evaluate them.

A number of scholars recently have been interested in the origins of the Badarian culture. Since there is no archeological evidence concerning the cultures that preceded the Badarian in Upper Egypt, and no evidence of Badarian or Badarian-like cultures anywhere else, this question is totally speculative. Nevertheless, interest in it was aroused when Anthony J. Arkell found a series of cultures in the Sudan containing pottery that was combed, incised, and impressed. In one of the later cultures, now called the Khartoum Neolithic, he found brown pottery decorated with blackened rims, possibly, Arkell suggested, in imitation of a cup made from a gourd that had been charred open. Arkell took the stand that pottery was invented only once and argued that since the earliest Sudanese pottery was simpler than that found in Egypt, it was probably older (Arkell and Ucko 1965:149–150). He also argued that the Badarian black-topped and rippled pottery probably originated in this culture. Baumgartel (1965:11) has followed Arkell's lead by suggesting that the Badarian culture originated in the south—a conclusion that is the more agreeable because it fits in with the general notion that the substratum of Egyptian culture is in some unidentified way "African," while the cultural development seen in Amratian and Gerzean times is the result of influences coming in from Southwest Asia.

A few resemblances in pottery types constitute slender evidence of a genetic relationship between two cultures. The problem is compounded (but the opportunity for speculation vastly increased) when virtually no archeological data are available for the entire region between Khartoum and Upper Egypt and when the cultural chronology of the Sudan is not sufficiently well worked out or correlated with that of Upper Egypt so that the Khartoum Neolithic (or Shaheinab) culture can be dated with accuracy. Arkell has guess-dated it around 3900 B.C., largely because he assumes that it had to precede the Badarian. The two C^{14} dates for·the site, however, are approximately 3100 and 3500 B.C., which are about the same as dates obtained for the Gerzean culture. This synchronism between the Khartoum Neolithic and Gerzean cultures is strengthened by certain close parallels in black-incised pottery and also by the fact that dwarf goats occur in the Gerzean site of Tukh as they do in the Khartoum Neolithic, where they are the earliest domestic animals known in the Sudan. There is also evidence that the Khartoum Neolithic site of Shaheinab was inhabited during a period of declining rainfall, probably after the climax of the Neolithic West Phase (Trigger 1965:58–59). While none of these arguments is sufficient to confirm a Gerzean date for the Khartoum Neolithic culture, they suggest that such a date is likely. They furthermore suggest that the traits common to both Shaheinab and the Badarian culture probably travelled from north to south, rather than in the opposite direction. In short, there is no solid evidence on which a southern origin of the Badarian culture or of any of its important characteristics can be based.

Brunton believed that there must have been some sort of cultural interruption between the end of the Badarian culture and the beginning of the Amratian, since the Badarian and later Predynastic graves that he found were always in different locations. This observation seems, however, to be merely the result of the small sample of Badarian sites that he examined and Gertrude Caton-Thompson, O. H. Myers, and others are of the opinion that there is a considerable "overlap" (that is, continuity) between the two cultures (Baumgartel 1965:14). Scarcely anyone now argues that a significant migration of people is needed to account for the development of the Amratian culture, and no one would take seriously Murray's (1951:3) theory that the coexistence of two races, indigene and invader, is suggested by the fact that some Amratian statuettes show people who are "tall, slender, and usually nude," others people who are short and often have a pointed beard. A cultural relationship between the Amratian culture and the Ghassulian of Palestine would account for similarities in ivory working, and Perrot has argued that there seems to be some sort of interconnection between Upper Egypt and Palestine both at this time and earlier. Kantor (1965:7) points out, however, that the tenuousness of the resemblances, as well as the absence of any more definite proofs of contact, urge caution with such arguments. Baumgartel (1947:54–71) has suggested that the White Cross-lined ware of the Amratian culture may have been inspired by the painted pottery found in Susa I and contemporary Mesopotamian and Iranian cultures. The designs on this Amratian pottery seem to be mainly of Egyptian origin, however, and the specific similarities with Asian pottery, which Baumgartel interprets as evidence of an historical connection, are in fact very general; hence few scholars accept her arguments. The absence of painted pottery in the Delta seems particularly fatal to an Asian origin for the Amratian painted pottery.

In spite of the lack of conclusive evidence of Southwest Asian influence in the Badarian and Amratian cultures, the possibility of such influence is not remote. Certain general similarities between the cultures of the Delta and Southwest Asia suggest the likelihood of cultural connections between Palestine and the Nile Valley. Moreover, the distance between these two regions is not great and during the Neolithic Wet Phase travel across the Sinai Peninsula was probably easier than it is today. Someday trade goods may be discovered and closer parallels worked out between the Egyptian and Palestinian cultures, that will demonstrate such connections. Once this has been done, we will be able to estimate better whether similarities further afield, such as those between Amratian and Mesopotamian stone vessels are the result of historical connections or are merely parallel developments. The distance between Cairo and Baghdad is less than 800 miles and, even if one has to travel through Syria to avoid the Arabian Desert, distance alone is unlikely to have prevented contact between the Egyptians and Mesopotamians.

The growing evidence of foreign contacts during the Gerzean period has helped to keep alive the idea that there was an important influx of foreigners, either at the start of this period or throughout it. Murray (1951:5–6) has suggested that the club mace gave the invaders superiority over the Amratians and that this allowed the "Gerzean people" to conquer and rule Upper Egypt. Baumgartel

(1965:21) writes that a foreign people with an urge to develop and spread first may have come as traders, and then, tempted by the riches of the Nile Valley, decided to settle there. Curiously enough (considering her views about the ecology of the Delta), she suggests that these people may have settled in the north before pushing on to conquer Upper Egypt. Kantor (1965:7) notes that in the early Gerzean phase (S.D. 50–65), there seems to have been increasing direct contact with foreign regions, since imported pottery and other objects become common at that time. The earlier influences include wavy ledge-handled jars, decorated pots with lug handles, and vessels with tilted spouts. The first of these seem to be of Palestinian, the latter two of Syrian and ultimately Mesopotamian origin. Once adopted by the Egyptians, these vessels evolved along lines different from those followed by the ancestral forms in Palestine (Vandier 1952:318–327). In the late Gerzean period the wavy-handled vessels became slimmer and the handles, originally functional, were reduced to a vestigial scallop decoration. Curiously enough, these later vessels are often decorated with a net pattern applied in red paint, which seems to be of Early Bronze Age I origin in Palestine and diffused to Egypt later than the original wavy-handled vessels. Kantor (1965:8) suggests, and her interpretation is in keeping with the canons of interpretation suggested in Chapter 4, that these influences appear to indicate "rather intensive outside connections, though probably not any large-scale foreign immigrations." Arkell and Ucko (1965:153) agree that "there is no evidence for any invasion [or of] a complete break with Amratian because Asiatic people invaded the Nile Valley [at this time]."

A number of items indicates contact, either direct or indirect, between Egypt and Mesopotamia in the late Gerzean phase. Three pots and four cylinder seals have been found in Egypt that appear to have actually been made in Mesopotamia. In addition, there are a number of artistic motifs which were adopted by Egyptian artists at this time and which seem to be of Mesopotamian origin. These include certain high-prowed ships, interlacing serpents, serpent necked panthers, a man dominating two animals (sometimes called the Gilgamesh or hero motif), a horizontal winged griffin, and the Mesopotamian headdresses and robes portrayed on some figures (Frankfort 1956:121–137). Kantor (1965:10–11) suggests that this material indicates a close temporal correlation between the late Gerzean and the late Protoliterate B and early Protoliterate C cultures in Mesopotamia. This also suggests that the diffusion of Mesopotamian items of culture took place during a relatively brief interval of time and possibly quite directly.

A major problem is the route along which these traits could have diffused. One possibility is through Syria and across the Sinai Peninsula; another by way of the Red Sea and along the Wadi Hammamat into Upper Egypt. The latter theory was in part suggested, and believed supported, by the discovery of high-prowed ship motifs among the rock pictures in the Eastern Desert, particularly along the Wadi Hammamat. To Winkler and others, these ships seem to mark the route along which foreign traits and people entered Egypt at this time. It is known, however, that the Egyptians used this route in early times and, consequently, there is no proof that these traits, whether or not of foreign origin, did not diffuse from the Nile Valley instead of in the opposite direction. Moreover, the people shown riding in these boats often wear feathers in their hair and appear to be natives of North Africa, most likely Egyptians. The boat motif is a widespread one in the Eastern and Western deserts and seems to have had a religious significance. Arkell (1959:52–53) has suggested that the idea of an association between gods and boats may ultimately be of Mesopotamian origin. Perhaps it spread from Southwest Asia throughout much of North Africa. The diffusion of this symbol may have accompanied the spread of domestic goats and cattle throughout the Sahara during the Neolithic Wet Phase.

Kantor (1965:11–14) supports the Red Sea route, although on the basis of other evidence. She points out that the Mesopotamian traits we have been considering have all been found in Upper Egypt, whereas Palestinian, but not Mesopotamian, traits are common at Maadi in the north. She also argues that Mesopotamian traits are less common in Palestine than they are in Egypt and that Protoliterate influence was apparently strong only in the Amuq and in the northern Orontes Valley, but not in other parts of Syria and Palestine. Because of this, it is impossible to demonstrate an overland route along which these traits could have traveled. Finally, the rapid transmission indicated by the close correlation between the late Gerzean context in which the traits were found and the Protoliterate B and C cultures, suggests a sea route rather than a more tenuous one overland. The sea route is also suggested by some renderings of ships in Egypt which are "overwhelmingly similar to Mesopotamian ones" (p. 12).

It should be noted that there is no more direct evidence of a route by sea than there is of one by land. In addition, the obvious difficulty of finding archeological evidence of sea travel constitutes only an uncomfortable negative argument in favor of this method of dispersal. Until exploration along the coast of Arabia and the Red Sea provides evidence of Protoliterate travellers or way stations, the Red Sea route must remain suspect. Moreover, it is not impossible that the royal court of the developing Upper Egyptian state was a promising market for Mesopotamian traders and perhaps even for Mesopotamian craftsmen, while there was relatively little that attracted their attention in Palestine. Similar courts may have existed in the Delta, but Maadi, a peripheral town, may not have been one of them. It is thus possible that Mesopotamian influences are found only in a limited area of Upper Egypt because of social and political factors rather than because of simple geography. A perhaps analogous situation is found in Nubia between 2000 and 1600 B.C. At that time little in the way of Egyptian material is found in the north, which was a poor region. Farther south, however, at Kerma, the Egyptians traded with one of the kings of Nubia who seems to have controlled the trade routes to the south. Vast amounts of Egyptian manufactured goods have been found there, produced in both a purely Egyptian style and one adapted to local tastes (W. S. Smith 1958:119). These, no doubt, were goods that the Egyptians gave in exchange for products from the south. It is not impossible, although it has not been proved, that the gold from the deserts of Upper Egypt already was attracting Asian traders in Predynastic times.

It is conceivable that as the kings of Upper Egypt grew more powerful, their taste for luxury goods was whetted and they began to employ skilled foreign artisans to turn out items conforming to local taste. The presence of these craftsmen in turn may have encouraged a higher standard of performance among local workmen. The handle of the Gebel el Arak knife, which on one side shows a definitely Mesopotamian figure dominating two animals, has been interpreted as depicting a battle between Egyptians and foreign invaders on the other (Vandier 1952:533–539; see also Figure 1 below). While the boats shown in the third register do look like the Mesopotamian vessels called *belems,* all of the combatants (although perhaps differentiated by long and short hair styles) are wearing the same sort of costume and one that does not appear to be un-Egyptian. This knife handle may be an object turned out by a Mesopotamian, or Mesopotamian-inspired, craftsman, who used local and foreign motifs to represent some purely local event or ritual.

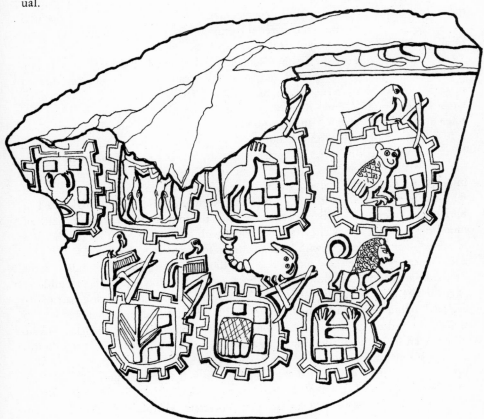

Figure 1. The Gebel el Arak knife-handle.

The Gerzean period was once described as a time of cultural stagnation. The point of this argument was that the unification of Egypt and the subsequent development of Early Dynastic civilization did not come about from internal development, but rather from the invasion of Egypt by a new and more progressive race. In his most recent work on Early Dynastic Egypt, Emery (1961:38–42) has repeated this claim, combining Derry's physical anthropological studies with his own vaguely expressed opinion that there are major discontinuities between the Gerzean and Early Dynastic cultures.

It is clear, however, that these "cultural discontinuities" have been greatly exaggerated (Kantor in Kraeling and Adams 1960:155–156). The differences between the Gerzean and Early Dynastic cultures seem to be mainly a product of the increasing social and cultural complexity that accompanied the unification of Egypt. These trends were to continue through Early Dynastic times and were to culminate, about 300 years later, in the brilliant achievements of the Old Kingdom. During the Early Dynastic period, traits continued to diffuse from Southwest Asia, but there was a growing tendency for Egyptian culture to develop a style of its own, which transformed these borrowings and made them thoroughly Egyptian. It is also apparent that most of the traits that are distinctive of Early Dynastic culture are part of the culture of the royal court, which evolved under the patronage of the new central government. By comparison, the material culture of the peasantry shows strong continuities with the past (Emery 1961:111).

Among the artistic accomplishments of the period of unification is a number of slate votive (?)[12] palettes and stone maceheads. In the scenes depicted on these objects we can see the canons of Egyptian official art developing over a relatively brief period of time. A mace of the so-called king "Scorpion"[13] shows this ruler in full regalia opening an irrigation canal. He is aided by an official who holds a basket to remove the earth for him. On the palettes of his presumed successor, King Narmer, the king is no longer aided by anyone, but is an aloof figure presiding at rituals or solemnly smiting his foes and triumphing over his defeated enemies. At Sakkara and Abydos a series of royal funerary monuments has been found which appear to begin in the reign of King Narmer. These monuments consist of burial and offering chambers covered with a rectangular superstructure built of mud-bricks. Those at Sakkara were decorated with a panelled brick facade that was plastered over and painted with bright patterns to resemble mat hangings. The plan and exterior niches of these tombs resemble those of Mesopotamian temples of the Protoliterate period. In Mesopotamia, however, the prototypes of these buildings begin in the Ubaid period (c. 4000 B.C.), and they remain an enduring part of the regional architectural tradition. In Egypt, brick panelling begins about the time of unification and disappears by the Second Dynasty. Some have argued that this panelling is an independent development, since the brick work does not resemble that of Mesopotamia in every detail. Most Egyptologists agree, however, that it is of Mesopotamian origin. Another trait that appears about the time of unification is writing. This begins with the use of ideographs to represent people's names, but soon more complicated inscriptions appear. It is uncertain whether the Egyptian system

---

[12] *Votive:* It has been suggested that these palettes were manufactured specifically as temple offerings. Although many of them have been found in temple contexts, this conclusion remains uncertain.

[13] The name of this Predynastic ruler is written with the hieroglyph of a Scorpion; the Egyptian pronunciation of the name is uncertain. Since this book was written Elise Baumgartel has published an inconclusive paper challenging the existence of King Scorpion. She dates the mace to Dynasty I and sees the Scorpion sign as a reference to a deity. She also chooses to interpret the scene on the mace as showing the king laying the foundations of a temple. It is hard to see how the winding trench or waterway shown on the lower half of the mace supports the latter part of her interpretation. See Elise Baumgartel, "Scorpion and Rosette and the Fragment of the Large Hierakonpolis Mace Head," *Zeitschrift für Ägyptische Sprache und Altertumskunde*, Vol. 92 (1966), 9–14.

of writing was an independent invention or the result of stimulus diffusion from Mesopotamia (Pope 1966). It appears, however, that if it were the latter, the idea of writing diffused, but little, if anything, in the way of details. While it is possible that some idea of writing (as opposed to any particular writing system) diffused from Mesopotamia to Egypt at this time, it would be notoriously difficult to prove it.

In terms of the criteria cited in Chapter 4, we can make the following general observations about cultural development in Predynastic times:

(1) Cultural development in Upper Egypt is characterized by continuity from Badarian times into the historic period. There is no evidence of any cultural break that would suggest the complete replacement of one population by another.

(2) There is also no evidence of changes in the physical characteristics of the population that would suggest a large and rapid influx of foreigners into Egypt at any time in the Predynastic period. This does not rule out the possibility of more casual gene flow nor does it assure that evidence of major changes in population in certain areas may not be forthcoming in the future. There is, however, at present, no physical anthropological evidence of any movements of people in Predynastic times, let alone of ones that were of culture historical significance. It is also likely, although it cannot be proved, that the population of most of Egypt was Egyptian-speaking, at least from Badarian times on. This conclusion is based on the evidence that Egyptian was a separate language by 5500 B.C., on the lack of evidence that it was ever spoken outside the Nile Valley, and on the strong evidence of physical and cultural continuities in Upper Egypt.

(3) So far, no intrusive sites have been found that could be attributed to immigrants entering Egypt. This, however, may be because of the small amount of archeological work that has been done. It becomes purely gratuitous to assume, in the absence of such evidence, that any innovations were introduced into the mainstream of Egyptian culture by organized groups of migrants who mingled with the local population. All theories of conquests by "master races," or the arrival of large organized groups of migrants, are as yet without foundation. Anyone wishing to sustain such arguments is required to find intrusive sites and show how, and whence, their inhabitants entered Egypt, and how the traits they brought with them became part of the mainstream of Egyptian culture.

(4) It is impossible to tell to what degree innovations entered Egypt solely as a result of trait diffusion (probably resulting largely from trade) and to what degree there was a settlement of individual foreigners, who introduced various innovations and brought new skills with them. The important point is that, whether or not foreigners settled in Egypt at this time, the traits that entered the country, whether in material culture, belief or language, found a place in the ongoing stream of cultural development. A model that stresses the essential continuity in people and traditions, accompanied by a diffusion of traits from Southwest Asia that were fitted into this continuum, seems to fit best the existing evidence.

(5) All of these conclusions are based on existing evidence and may be refined or modified as more evidence accumulates. The careful excavation of living sites may resolve whether or not an influx of settlers accompanied the diffusion of Asian traits into Egypt in Gerzean times. Evidence may even be found of limited

organized migration. It is unlikely, however, that such discoveries will greatly upset the existing picture of ethnic and cultural continuity.

Social and Political Development

Having reviewed the record of cultural development, it is necessary to examine Predynastic Egypt from a social and political point of view to see if the proposed sequence makes sense within this frame of reference as well. When we try to do this, the shortcomings in the archeological record become still more apparent. We have devoted considerable space to the unresolved dispute concerning the relative state of cultural development in the Delta and in Upper Egypt and noted various claims that the Delta was more advanced, less advanced, or at about the same stage of development as the south. As long as no archeological evidence is available concerning the prehistory of major centers in the Delta, there will be large gaps in our knowledge of Egypt. Even in the Upper Egypt, where more evidence is available, there are good reasons to suspect the reliability of the picture of social conditions that is derived from the cemeteries and encampments found along the edge of the desert. Future work at major sites, like Hierakonpolis, may compel us to modify the idea that the social structure of the early Predynastic cultures was simple and relatively unstratified and that the only settlements at that time were small ones of farmers living in reed huts. The main evidence which supports the current view of these cultures is the general lack of differentiation in grave types and the absence of notable foreign contacts.

It has been suggested that in early Predynastic times each village was autonomous and had a chief whose power rested on his reputation as a "rainmaker-king" (Frankfort 1948:18,33–35). Rainmakers have been found among African tribes such as the Dinka, Chungu, and Jukun in recent times and in some of these tribes they were killed when it was believed that their magical powers had begun to wane. The validity of such an analogy between modern African customs and those of ancient Egypt rests for the most part on the unproved assumption that Predynastic practices diffused to the upper reaches of the Nile, and have survived there to the present day; or, that the Egyptian and Nilotic cultures both grew out of a common cultural substratum (Seligman and Murray 1911; Blackman 1916). It might be noted in passing that the use of the term "rainmaker" is an anomoly, since even if there was considerably more precipitation in Egypt in Predynastic times than there is today, it is unlikely that rainmaking was of much importance to the Egyptians. Most of the people who use this term are quick to point out that such chiefs were probably believed able to control the Nile flood, on which the prosperity of the valley depended.

The basis of this idea was an ancient Egyptian rite, celebrated in historic times well-on in a king's reign, in which the Pharaoh symbolically died and was reborn. The *Sed* festival is often stated by Egyptologists to be a late version of a ritual that in Predynastic times involved the sacrifice of the chief, and those who read Seligman's ethnographic accounts of the Sudan have compared this rite with the ritual regicide reported among the Shilluk and other groups. In actual fact, there is no direct evidence that chiefs were ever slain in this manner in Predynastic times or that they were rainmakers or any other kind of magicians. The two Gerzean graves that, rather tenuously, have been interpreted as those of sorcerers appear to have been those of women (Baumgartel 1965:34).

In apparent contrast with preceding periods, the Gerzean was one of rapidly developing technology, frequent contact with foreign regions, heightened social differentiation, and the growing power and organization of the state. A scene on the Tjehnu palette (if interpreted correctly) suggests that fortified towns or castles of local chiefs (it is not clear which) were common at this time and there are many other pictorial representations which suggest a good deal of warfare. It appears that states began to emerge and soon began to compete with one another. How many of these there were and the history of their conflicts remain unknown. The cause of their coming into being is likewise obscure, but it may have been a response in part to a developing subsistence economy and in part to growing trade and contact with Southwest Asia. Since Egypt at this time was culturally less developed than Southwest Asia, these contacts may have been quite influential, but while they may help to explain the cultural background for the political developments that took place, they do not explain why political power so quickly became centralized in Egypt instead of finding its locus in a network of city states. This was something quite different from anything known in Southwest Asia and probably came about because rapid cultural development (involving some outside stimuli) led to the creation of a large conquest state before strong regional institutions and loyalties could emerge from the earlier tribal or village system. Many close structural parallels probably can be found between the development of the Egyptian state and that of more recent conquest states such as the Zulu Empire.

There is also the question of why a southern state should have been the one to unite all of Egypt. If Kantor's Red Sea theory is correct, cultural advantages derived through direct contact with Mesopotamia may offer a partial explanation. Local access to supplies of gold, and perhaps copper, in the south may be another reason and Baumgartel (1965:20) has laid stress on the fact that the ancient name of the town of Naqada was Nubet, which may mean "the town of Gold."

It is perhaps more significant that the reunification of Egypt at the start of the Middle and New Kingdoms was in both instances accomplished by rulers who came from Upper Egypt. Southern rulers appear to have been able to recruit good bowmen among the Nubians and Beja to the south and were able to push their way north through the Nile Valley, disposing of one rival at a time, until they were able to master the Delta. Rulers in the Delta, on the other hand, had to compete with several neighbors at a time. Thus geopolitical considerations may have made the south a considerably better region to start building a kingdom than either Middle Egypt or the Delta. The old theory that royal power was based on the dependence of a growing population on irrigation and drainage works that required a central government for their management, is no longer tenable. The mace of King Scorpion shows him digging an irrigation canal and a late legend claims that it was Menes, the first king of Egypt, who built a dam to protect Memphis from the floods, but there is little evidence that the central government was directly concerned with local irrigation works in pharaonic times (R. M. Adams 1960a:280–286). Nims

(1965:34) has pointed out that the basin irrigation that was used in the Nile Valley until fairly recent times did not depend on well-developed central control. What the kings of Egypt did organize was *corvée* labor to undertake large works of construction, as well as the careful assessing of lands as a basis for computing taxes. These activities, however, are a consequence rather than a cause of the development of royal power.

Much speculation concerning specific historical events in the unification of Egypt has been based on the elaborately decorated palettes and mace heads that were produced at the end of the Gerzean period and at the beginning of the First Dynasty (Vandier 1952:570–605). Some of the latest of these bear the names of king Narmer and the presumed King "Scorpion." Narmer is definitely attested as a king of Upper and Lower Egypt, but "Scorpion," his supposed predecessor, appears only as a king of Upper Egypt, unless Arkell (1963) is correct when he reads his name on a much damaged mace head showing a king wearing the red crown of Lower Egypt. The scenes associated with these two kings show them triumphing over their enemies, celebrating rituals, and opening canals or irrigation ditches.

Other palettes depict hunting and battle scenes and animals, but are not associated with any king. These are mostly assumed to date from a time before royal power was clearly defined or names were written in hieroglyphs. The so-called "hunter's palette," on which the hunters and their quarry are assymetrically arranged, is believed solely on stylistic grounds to be one of the earliest. Few of these palettes were found in satisfactory stratigraphic contexts, hence their proposed chronological sequence is based on stylistic criteria and is far from certain. This immediately diminishes the historical value of these objects.

It generally has been assumed that the scenes depicting people or battles celebrate particular historical events and that the palettes can be interpreted as historical documents. Some of the events depicted are admittedly obscure, but it is maintained, for example, that the Narmer palette, which shows that king smiting an enemy from the marsh lands, commemorates the conquest of the Delta. The fact that the king is shown on the same palette as a bull smiting what appears to be an Asian must raise the question whether the palette commemorates any one specific event or whether it is merely a statement of royal power.

The interpretation of the "earlier" palettes presents even greater problems. The fragmentary "Libyan palette" (Fig. 2) has a scene depicting various birds and animals hacking away at a number of strong rectangular walls. It is debated whether the latter are forts or towns, and whether they represent specific localities or are symbols used for districts. Likewise, it is uncertain whether they represent a number of different places or are all synonyms for one place, such as the northern city of Buto. It is also uncertain whether the figures attacking the town represent a confederacy of clans or districts, various gods that helped a king to victory, or whether they are all symbolic representations of the king. It is clear that if experts cannot agree on the interpretation of basic features such as these, the overall significance of these representations will remain in doubt.

Similar but more serious problems of interpretation beset efforts to trace the activities of clans, districts, or small states, using the various ensigns that appear on the painted pottery of the Gerzean period, often in association with the boats depicted on this pottery. There is no doubt that some of these insignia are symbols of gods that are known in historic times, and there is no reason to doubt that these gods were worshipped in the Predynastic period. The attempt, however, to see each god or insignia as the patron of a particular district creates many difficulties (Vandier 1952:340–342) and overlooks the likelihood that all of this pottery was produced in a very limited number of localities. The symbols of no particular god appear restricted to any one place and deities later associated with the north occur in the south. It is likely that in Gerzean times, just as later, many gods were worshipped throughout Egypt although they might have a cult center in a particular region. Hence any effort to read a political significance into these symbols appears hazardous. What significance they do have, and whatever associations are found among them, are more likely to be of a purely religious and mythological character.

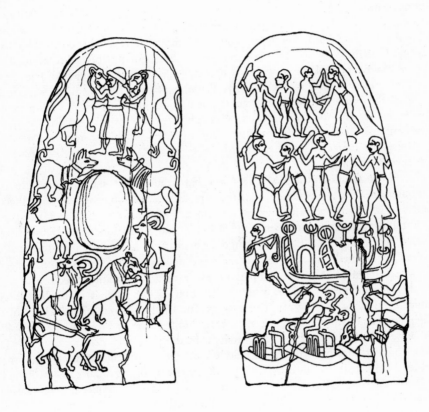

Figure 2. The obverse side of the so-called Libyan palette.

Whatever the impetus involved, the Thinite kings appear to have gained control of Egypt in no more than a few generations and their power for a time may have extended into Nubia and Palestine as well (Yeivin 1965). Although conquest was an important factor in the growth of the state, its development probably depended also on alliances between the kings and local rulers, who were either allowed to remain in office in their former territory or else were given positions of importance in the new nationwide bureaucracy. Possibly the loyalty of the more important local rulers was secured through intermarriage with the royal family. Once in control of the surpluses and manpower of the whole country, the kings were able to support artisans and undertake building projects on an unprecedented scale. Indeed, because of the highly centralized nature of the national redistributive system that had developed by the start of the Old Kingdom, they were probably the only patrons in Egypt who could support such development. It is thus no wonder that the main cultural developments that followed unification, and led to the flowering of Egyptian civilization a few centuries later, were court centered phenomena. Egypt had been politically united while the country as a whole had remained at a fairly primitive level of economic and cultural development. With the emergence of a strong central government all of the nascent political and economic institutions throughout the country fell under royal control. Foreign trade appears to have been a royal monopoly and the best craftsmen were those in the employ of the state. As a result, all of the economic developments that in Mesopotamia helped to create urban centers, in Egypt took place within a national bureaucratic framework. The artistic and cultural accomplishments of Egypt throughout early historic times were reflections of the power of the central government and were designed for the benefit of the state gods and the upper classes. Through its control over the internal economy, over imports, and over craftsmen, the government was able to remain for a long time the sole source of material reward and by this means was able to control Egypt effectively.

Max Gluckman (1965:143–144) has argued that states created through conquest can only achieve stability if they are able to develop complex internal economies or if they participate in extensive foreign trade. Both of these factors can provide the organic unity, and hence the stability, that a unilateral state lacks. Viewed very schematically, the Egyptian kingdom appears to be a conquest state that acquired exceptional stability through the rapid development of occupational specialization, foreign trade, and a complex bureaucratic administration. Because so much of this development occurred after the creation of the state, it took place largely under royal aegis and control. This may explain the highly centralized nature of the Egyptian administration and the apparently limited participation of most people in the elite culture during the Old Kingdom. In the provincial cemeteries of the Old Kingdom practically nothing is reflected of the great architectural and artistic achievements that we now regard as the hallmark of Egyptian civilization. The fruits of Mesopotamian civilization were divided among a number of city states and among numerous citizens within each of these urban centers. By contrast, the fruits of Egyptian civilization were expended on the royal court and to a very large degree, as the construction of the royal mortuary complexes shows, on the person of the king. Early Mesopotamia created nothing on the scale of the Egyptian pyramids, but a greater number of Mesopotamians probably benefitted from, and participated in, the Great Tradition of their society than did their Egyptian counterparts. As a court civilization growing out of conquest, Old Kingdom Egypt appears in many ways to be structurally more similar to other unilateral states such as Dahomey or Buganda, than it does to the early civilizations of the Near East, whose cultural capital the Egyptians put to such good use.

7

Epilogue

A N INTEREST IN PREHISTORY requires no defense. It is generally recognized that understanding man's past is an essential part of understanding his behavior at the present time and that any general explanation of human development must be answerable to the historical record.

Because the prehistorian works without written records, his methods resemble those used by paleontologists and historical geologists. Each of these disciplines seeks both to reconstruct the past and to explain the changes that can be observed in the historical record. Much of the evidence that they use consists of the remains of the past, be these geological strata, organic fossils, or the artifacts and debris of ancient cultures. Additional evidence is found in the conditions of the present, on the basis of which past conditions may be inferred. Each of these disciplines attempts to utilize many independent lines of evidence to reconstruct the past, and when the conclusions based on these different approaches converge, greater certainty in the validity of the reconstruction is achieved.

Prehistory differs from the natural sciences in that the object of its investigation is man and his works. Therefore any explanation of how changes take place must be based on a sound understanding of human behavior. This accounts for the close relationship between prehistory and the social sciences, in particular with cultural anthropology.

Prehistory is concerned with all aspects of human development. Like documentary history, it is interested in delineating and explaining social, economic, political, and demographic, as well as cultural changes. Racial and linguistic changes are also objects of interest. In this way prehistory becomes a meeting place of many disciplines, such as archeology, culture history, and historical linguistics.

The study of prehistory, either in general or in any particular region of the world, takes the form of a dialogue between the evidence, be it archeological, physical anthropological, or linguistic, and the social science theories that are used to interpret it. The discovery of new evidence frequently requires the modification of existing historical reconstructions; on the other hand, theoretical advances also permit new insights to be gained from existing data and this too results in the elaboration and modification of such reconstructions. In the case of Predynastic Egypt, we have seen that the evidence, derived largely from cemeteries, is inadequate to answer many of the problems about social and political development that a growing theoretical interest in these problems has raised. Theoretical advances thus also lead archeological (and linguistic) studies to develop along wholly new lines.

Until recently, the theories that prehistorians used to interpret evidence tended to be largely informal and implicit. Methodology was concerned largely with excavation techniques and the interpretation of archeological data for site reports. This is sometimes referred to as a descriptive period. In the past few years, however, prehistorians have been paying increasing attention to making their techniques of historical reconstruction and interpretation explicit. This development is indicative of the maturation of prehistory as a discipline.

One of the earliest theoretical advances in prehistory was the recognition that race, language, and culture are independent variables, each of which must be examined separately and in terms of its own evidence. Although anthropologists have long realized that race, language, and culture each change according to their own rules and that the history of each is apt to follow a distinctive course, the tendency to think in terms of racial and ethnic stereotypes has made the application of this very difficult.

Still more difficult has been the realization that prehistoric cultures are not merely collections of traits, to be compared in terms of their overall similarities and differences, but rather systems in which each trait has played a particular role. This view, which has already gained wide acceptance, has done much to weaken the tendency to treat archeological cultures as organic bounded units. It is also permitting prehistorians to distinguish between the study of individual traits, their origin and diffusion, and the study of the development of social systems, within which cultural traits come to play a part. Related to this interest in social systems, is the increasing attention being shown to the study of prehistoric settlement patterns.

Within the context of these developments, serious attention once again is being given to the processes of cultural change. In the past, the processes of invention, diffusion, and migration were invoked in a careless and uncritical manner as explanations of culture change. Today these concepts are being reassessed and criteria are being established for distinguishing them in the archeological record.

Hopefully, the theoretical developments now going on in prehistory are preparing the way for an enriched and more sophisticated understanding of man's past. Just as in the discipline of history, so in prehistory, there is no single line of investigation to be followed. Instead, all of man's achievements in all areas of human endeavor lie open for investigation. For the prehistorian, contact with these achievements is limited because prehistoric peoples cannot speak to us directly through their records. Archeological remains are not culture, they are only the products of culture. Moreover they are imperfect reflections of the culture that produced them, just as organic fossils are an incomplete version of a living animal. The interest and importance of prehistory lie not in the completeness of the records of the past, nor in the theoretical skills that are at our disposal to interpret these records. Its strength derives instead from man and his achievements both in the past and today. Imperfect as the record may be, it still leaves us with many kingdoms of the human spirit to explore.

Selected Bibliography
of Methodological Works

[References for all works cited in this section are given in the General Bibliography. This section is a guide to important readings, not a comprehensive bibliography or a recapitulation of references cited in the text.]

Like its mother-discipline of history, prehistory has been oriented more towards practice than toward theory. Its methodological literature is less extensive and less well formulated than that of archeology, and very often its subject matter appears as a small section in works that are devoted to the latter discipline. Until recently, the premises on which the interpretation of prehistory is based have largely been implicit and few attempts have been made to formulate procedures. Because of this, methodology often must be disentangled from works that are not methodologically oriented. When reading site reports and general works on prehistory, the student should constantly attempt to note carefully and evaluate the concepts that underly the interpretations being offered.

The one exception to this dearth of methodological material is the field of culture history, in its narrowest sense of making historical inferences on the basis of distributional data. Many of these articles, however, are of a polemical nature and frequently repeat the same arguments with no new insights or additional documentation. For this reason, only a representative sample of these articles is noted.

CHAPTER I

For a discussion of historical method see Nagel 1961, Chapter 15; for the relationship between history and anthropology, Evans-Pritchard 1962. The development of prehistory is traced in Daniel 1963. For general discussions of methods see Ehrich 1950; Clark 1953; Rouse 1953; Willey 1953*b*; C. Hawkes 1954; MacWhite 1956; Piggott 1961; 1965 (introduction); and W. W. Taylor 1948. Note that American writers frequently do not distinguish between archeology and prehistory.

CHAPTER II

For a discussion of the independence of race, language, and culture see Sapir 1921:121–235 and the essays in Boas 1940.

The most sophisticated works in the field of prehistory at the present time seem mostly to be concerned with Africa. The best booklength discussion of what may be called the "synthetic approach" to prehistory is McCall 1964. Although concerned with African prehistory, the points that McCall makes are applicable anywhere. For shorter general treatments of the sorts of information that are of use to a prehistorian see Murdock 1959a:1–47 and Vansina 1965:173–182. For discussions of various problems involved in using these kinds of data see the recent issues of the *Journal of African History*. For an exemplary synthetic approach to Polynesian prehistory see Suggs 1960.

Descriptions of archeological techniques and of methods of interpreting archeological data are found in standard texts such as Wheeler 1954; Piggot 1959; Kenyon 1961; De Laet 1957; Hole and Heizer 1965. Selected readings from site reports are found in Heizer 1959. Many articles of methodological interest are contained in Brothwell and Higgs 1963. References to distributional studies are given in part 4, below.

The principal study of the use of oral traditions is Vansina 1965. Additional references can be found in that book.

No current work adequately summarizes the role of physical anthropology in prehistoric studies. For a survey of some of the problems involved in trying to reconstruct racial history see Garn 1962. Livingstone 1958 provides an example of the use of a multidisciplinary approach to reconstructing the history of one genetic trait.

The classic study of the role of linguistics in prehistory is Sapir 1916. For a discussion of recent distributional studies see Dyen 1956 and for a model study of diffusion using linguistic data see Greenberg 1960. For a discussion of the use of linguistic data to reconstruct ancient cultures see Thieme 1964, Friedrich 1966. There is a discussion of the role of linguistics in prehistory in MacGaffey 1966. Palmer 1965 (especially pages 184–211) has written a valuable study of the use of archeological and linguistic data in the reconstruction of prehistory.

CHAPTER III

For discussions of the concept of culture in anthropology see Tallgren 1937; Binford 1962; Caldwell 1966. Methodological literature dealing with the concepts of society and culture as applied in prehistory is fairly scarce. The separation of the two concepts was implicit in Childe's (1951) distinction between social and cultural evolution and can also be noted in the different manner in which he treated the data in *The Prehistory of European Society* (1958) and in *The Dawn of European Civilization* (1939). Theoretically, however, Childe did little to distinguish these two concepts. The present interest in social systems as systems is evident in recent papers such as Longacre 1964; 1966.

One of the best systematic treatments of the correlations that have been made between social and cultural units is found in MacWhite 1956. Other references to this problem can be found in the text.

For a discussion of the need to understand function in order to interpret archeological data see Steward and Setzler 1938; W. W. Taylor 1948; Sonnenfeld 1962. Also see Lowie 1912 on premature classification.

CHAPTER IV

The best general treatments of invention, diffusion and migration are found in Linton 1936, Kroeber 1948, and R. B. Dixon 1928. These works review numerous examples, contain an extensive critique of earlier works and provide many bibliographic references.

Invention is also discussed in Steward 1929; Gibson 1948 and H. C. Moore 1954; invention and diffusion in Rogers 1962; Service 1964. For the methodology of the Vienna School see Schmidt 1939 and Kluckhohn 1936; for age-area theory Wissler 1917, 1923, 1927; Spier 1921 and Kroeber 1931. For survivals see Lowie 1918 and Hodgen 1931. There is a vast literature on discontinuous distributions. References and critiques for the major studies can be found in Kroeber 1949 and R. B. Dixon 1928. The chapter entitled "Historic Reconstructions" in Linton 1936 is worthy of special note. Many of the more recent studies have been largely inconclusive re-examinations of the original problem cases. Erasmus 1950, for example, deals with the relationship between pachisi and patolli, first discussed by Tylor in 1879, and Riley 1952 reworks earlier data on the blow-gun (see R. B. Dixon 1928:121).

For a discussion of convergence and limited possibilities see Lowie 1912; Goldenweiser 1913; Rands 1956, 1961; Rands and Riley 1958; Harris and Morren 1966. Some miscellaneous recent studies of diffusion that are of special interest are Tolstoy 1953; K. A. Dixon 1964; Schroeder 1964 and Fraser 1966. For the comparison of large numbers of traits see Sturtevant 1960; Meggers 1964; Rowe 1966.

Radcliffe-Brown's (1958: Chapter 1) critique of distributional studies (which he calls ethnology) is of some historical interest.

For a collection of methodologically-oriented papers dealing with migrations in New World prehistory see Thompson 1958. Especially note Rouse's concluding paper, also Jett 1962. For other discussions of the relationship between movements of population and culture change see MacWhite 1956 and Palmer 1965.

CHAPTER V

Most references to papers dealing with the inference of social structure from prehistoric evidence are given in the text. For general works on the origin of complex societies see Lowie 1927; MacLeod 1924 and Coe 1961. For general expositions of the unilateral theory see Gumplowicz 1963; Oppenheimer 1914; for organic theories Morgan 1877; Engels 1962; Childe 1942; Steward 1955; Wittfogel 1957; White 1949.

CHAPTER VI

The most thorough digest of material on Predynastic Egypt, and a complete guide to the original reports is found in Vandier 1952. Unfortunately, this book is not available in an English translation. English syntheses of material on Predynastic Egypt are found in Childe 1934; Baumgartel 1947 and 1965; Gardiner 1961; Kantor 1965; Arkell and Ucko 1965 and (for northern Egypt only) in Hayes 1965. Information on Early Dynastic Egypt is readily available in Emery 1961 and Edwards 1964 and an excellent description of Egyptian social and political structure in historic times is included in Frankfort 1956.

General Bibliography

ADAMS, ROBERT M., 1960a, "Early Civilizations, Subsistence and Environment." C. H. Kraeling and R. M. Adams (eds.), *City Invincible*. Chicago: University of Chicago Press, pp. 269–295.

———, 1960b, "The Origin of Cities," *Scientific American*, 203, No. 3: 153–168.

———, 1966, *The Evolution of Urban Society: Early Mesopotamia and Prehispanic Mexico*. Chicago: Aldine Publishing Company.

ADAMS, WILLIAM Y., 1965, "Post-Pharaonic Nubia in the Light of Archaeology II." *Journal of Egyptian Archaeology*, 51:160–178.

ALDRED, CYRIL, 1965, *Egypt to the End of the Old Kingdom*. London: Thames and Hudson.

ARKELL, ANTHONY J., 1957, "Khartoum's Part in the Development of the Neolithic." *Kush*, 5:8–12.

———, 1959, "Early Shipping in Egypt." *Antiquity*, 33:52–53.

———, 1961, *A History of the Sudan from the Earliest Times to 1821*. London: Athlone Press.

———, 1963, "Was King Scorpion Menes?", *Antiquity*, 37:31–35.

ARKELL, ANTHONY J. and Peter J. Ucko, 1965, "Review of Predynastic Development in the Nile Valley." *Current Anthropology*, 6:145–66.

BASCOM, WILLIAM, 1955, "Urbanization Among the Yoruba." *American Journal of Sociology*, 60:446–454.

BATRAWI, AHMED, 1945–1946, "The Racial History of Egypt and Nubia." *Journal of the Royal Anthropological Institute*, 75:81–101; 76:131–56.

BAUMGARTEL, ELISE J., 1947, *The Cultures of Predynastic Egypt*, Vol. I, London: Oxford University Press. (rev. ed. 1955; Vol. II 1960).

———, 1965, "Predynastic Egypt" in *The Cambridge Ancient History*. Vol. I, fascicle 38.

BINFORD, LEWIS R., 1962, "Archaeology as Anthropology." *American Antiquity*, 28:217–225.

BLACKMAN, AYLWARD M., 1916, "Some Remarks on an Emblem upon the Head of an Ancient Egyptian Birth-Goddess." *Journal of Egyptian Archaeology*, 3:199–206.

BOAS, FRANZ, 1940, *Race, Language and Culture*. New York: The Macmillan Company.

BRACE, C. LORING, 1964, "The Fate of the Classic Neanderthals: a Consideration of Hominid Catastrophism." *Current Anthropology*, 5:3–43.

BROTHWELL, DON and ERIC HIGGS, 1963, *Science in Archaeology.* New York: Basic Books, Inc.

BUTZER, KARL W., 1959, "Die Naturlandschaft Ägyptens während der Vorgeschichte und der dynastischen Zeit." Abhandlungen der Akademie der Wissenschaften und der Literatur (Mainz). *Mathematische-Naturwissenschaftliche*, Klasse No. 2, 1–80.

————, 1960, "Archaeology and Geology in Ancient Egypt: Geomorphological Analysis Permits Reconstruction of the Geography of Prehistoric Settlement." *Science* 132:1617–1624.

————, 1964, *Environment and Archaeology: an Introduction to Pleistocene Geography.* Chicago: Aldine Publishing Company.

CALDWELL, JOSEPH R., 1966, "The New American Archaeology." Joseph R. Caldwell (ed.), *New Roads to Yesterday.* New York: Basic Books, pp. 333–347 (originally published in 1959, *Science,* 129:303–307).

CHANG, KWANG-CHIH, 1958, "Study of the Neolithic Social Grouping: Examples from the New World." *American Anthropologist,* 60:298–334.

————, 1962, "A Typology of Settlement and Community Patterns in Some Circumpolar Societies." *Arctic Anthropology,* 1:28–41.

CHILDE, V. GORDON, 1934, *New Light on the Most Ancient East: The Oriental Prelude to European Prehistory.* London: Routledge and Kegan Paul, Ltd.

————, 1939, *The Dawn of European Civilization,* 3d ed. London: Routledge and Kegan Paul, Ltd.

————, 1942, *What Happened in History.* Baltimore: Penguin Books Inc.

————, 1950, "The Urban Revolution." *Town Planning Review,* 21:3–17.

————, 1951, *Social Evolution.* New York: Abelard-Schuman, Ltd.

————, 1956, *Piecing Together the Past, the Interpretation of Archaeological Data.* London: Routledge and Kegan Paul, Ltd.

————, 1958, *The Prehistory of European Society.* Baltimore, Md.: Penguin Books, Inc.

CLARK, J. GRAHAME D., 1953, "Archeological Theories and Interpretation: Old World." A. L. Kroeber (ed.), *Anthropology Today.* Chicago: University of Chicago Press, pp. 343–360.

COE, MICHAEL D., 1957, "The Khmer Settlement Pattern: A Possible Analogy with that of the Maya." *American Antiquity,* 22:409–410.

————, 1961, "Social Typology and Tropical Forest Civilizations." *Comparative Studies in Society and History,* 4:65–85.

————, 1965, "A Model of Ancient Community Structure in the Maya Lowlands." *Southwestern Journal of Anthropology,* 21:97–114.

COON, CARLETON S., 1965, *The Living Races of Man.* New York: Alfred A. Knopf.

DALES, GEORGE F., 1964, "The Mythical Massacre at Mohenjodaro." Expedition 6.

DANIEL, GLYN, 1963, *The Idea of Prehistory.* Cleveland: The World Publishing Company.

DEETZ, JAMES, 1965, The Dynamics of Stylistic Change in Arikara Ceramics. Urbana: *Illinois Studies in Anthropology,* No. 4.

DERRY, D. E., 1956, "The Dynastic Race in Egypt." *Journal of Egyptian Archaeology,* 42:80–85.

DE LAET, SIGFRIED J., 1957, *Archaeology and its Problems.* London: Phoenix House Ltd.

DIXON, KEITH A., 1964, "The Acceptance and Persistence of Ring Vessels and Stirrup Spout-handles in the Southwest." *American Antiquity,* 29:455–460.

DIXON, ROLAND B., 1928, *The Building of Cultures.* New York: Charles Scribner's Sons.

DYEN, ISIDORE, 1956, "Language Distribution and Migration Theory." *Language,* 32: 611–626.

EDMONSON, MONRO, S., 1961, "Neolithic Diffusion Rates." *Current Anthropology,* 2:71–102.

EDWARDS, I. E. S., 1964, "The Early Dynastic Period in Egypt" in *The Cambridge Ancient History*, Vol. I, fascicle 25.

EHRICH, ROBERT W., 1950, "Some Reflections on Archaeological Interpretation." *American Anthropologist*, 52:468–482.

EKHOLM, GORDON F., 1964, "Transpacific Contacts." Jennings, Jesse D. and Edward Norbeck (eds.), *Prehistoric Man in the New World*. Chicago: University of Chicago Press, pp. 489–510.

EMERY, WALTER B., 1961, *Archaic Egypt*. Baltimore, Penguin Books, Inc.

ENGELS, FREDERICK, 1962, The Origin of the Family, Private Property and the State. Marx, Karl and Frederick Engels, *Selected Works*, Vol. II. Moscow: Foreign Languages Publishing House, pp. 170–327.

ERASMUS, CHARLES J., 1950, "Patolli and Pachisi, and the Limitation of Possibilities." *Southwestern Journal of Anthropology*, 6:369–387.

———, 1961, *Man takes Control*. Minneapolis: University of Minnesota Press.

EVANS-PRITCHARD, EDWARD E., 1962, "Anthropology and History." *Essays in Social Anthropology*. London: Faber & Faber, Ltd. pp. 46–65.

FALLERS, LLOYD A., 1964, "Social Stratification and Economic Processes." Melville J. Herskovits and M. Harwitz (eds.), *Economic Transition in Africa*. Evanston, Ill.: Northwestern University Press.

FEI, HSIAO-T'UNG, 1953, *China's Gentry: Essays in Rural-Urban Relations*. Chicago: University of Chicago Press.

FORDE, C. DARYLL, 1934, *Habitat, Economy and Society: a Geographical Introduction to Ethnology*. London: Methuen & Co., Ltd.

FRANKFORT, HENRI, 1948, *Kingship and the Gods*. Chicago: University of Chicago Press.

———, 1956, *The Birth of Civilization in the Near East*. New York: Doubleday & Company.

FRASER, DOUGLAS, 1966, "The Heraldic Woman: A Study in Diffusion." Douglas Fraser (ed.), *The Many Faces of Primitive Art*. Englewood Cliffs, N.J.: Prentice-Hall, Inc., pp. 36–99.

FRIEDRICH, PAUL, 1966, "Proto-Indo-European Kinship." *Ethnology*, 5:1–36.

GARDINER, ALAN, 1961, *Egypt of the Pharaohs*. Oxford: Oxford University Press.

GARN, STANLEY M., 1962, *Human Races*. Springfield, Ill.: Charles C Thomas, Publisher.

GIBSON, GORDON D., 1948, "The Probability of Numerous Independent Inventions." *American Anthropologist*, 50:362–364.

GIMBUTAS, MARIJA, 1963, "The Indo-Europeans: Archaeological Problems." *American Anthropologist*, 65:815–836.

GLUCKMAN, MAX, 1940, "The Kingdom of the Zulu of South Africa." Meyer Fortes and E. E. Evans-Pritchard (eds.), *African Political Systems*. London: Oxford University Press, pp. 25–55.

———, 1964, *Closed Systems and Open Minds: the Limits of Naivety in Social Anthropology*. Chicago: Aldine Publishing Company.

———, 1965, *Politics, Law and Ritual in Tribal Society*. Chicago: Aldine Publishing Company.

GOLDENWEISER, ALEXANDER A., 1913, "The Principle of Limited Possibilities." *Journal of American Folklore*, 26:259–292.

GOLDSCHMIDT, WALTER, 1959, *Man's Way*. New York: Holt, Rinehart and Winston, Inc.

GRAEBNER, FRITZ, 1911, *Methode der Ethnologie*. Heidelberg: C. Winter.

GREENBERG, JOSEPH H., 1955, *Studies in African Linguistic Classification*. New Haven, Conn. Compass Publishing Company.

———, 1957, *Essays in Linguistics*. Chicago: University of Chicago Press.

———, 1960, "Linguistic Evidence for the Influence of the Kanuri on the Hausa." *Journal of African History*, 1:205–212.

GRIFFITHS, J. GWYN, 1960, *The Conflict of Horus and Seth.* Liverpool: Liverpool University Press.

GUDSCHINSKY, SARAH C., 1956, "The ABC's of Lexicostatistics (glottochronology)." *Word,* 12:175–210.

GUMPLOWICZ, LUDWIG, 1963, *Outlines of Sociology.* Irving L. Horowitz (ed.). 2d English language edition. New York: Paine-Whitman.

HARRIS, MARVIN and G. E. B. MORREN, 1966, "The Limitations of the Principle of Limited Possibilities." *American Anthropologist,* 68:122–27.

HASELBERGER, HERTA, 1961, "Method of Studying Ethnological Art." *Current Anthropology,* 2:341–384.

HAWKES, CHRISTOPHER, 1954, "Archaeological Theory and Method: Some suggestions from the Old World." *American Anthropologist,* 56:155–68.

HAWKES, JACQUETTA and SIR LEONARD WOOLLEY, 1963, *Prehistory and the Beginnings of Civilization.* New York: Harper & Row, Publishers.

HAYES, WILLIAM C., 1965, *Most Ancient Egypt.* Chicago: University of Chicago Press.

HEIZER, ROBERT F., 1959, *The Archaeologist at Work: a Source Book in Archaeological Method and Interpretation.* New York: Harper & Row, Publishers.

———, (ed.), 1962, *Man's Discovery of his Past: Literary Landmarks in Archaeology.* Englewood Cliffs, N.J.: Prentice-Hall, Inc.

HILL, JAMES N., 1966, "A Prehistoric Community in Eastern Arizona." *Southwestern Journal of Anthropology* 22:9–30.

HODGEN, MARGARET T., 1931, "Doctrine of Survivals." *American Anthropologist,* 33:307–324.

———, 1952, Change and History. *Viking Fund Publications in Anthropology* 18.

HOLE, FRANK and ROBERT F. HEIZER, 1965, *An Introduction to Prehistoric Archeology.* New York: Holt, Rinehart and Winston, Inc.

HUGHES, GEORGE R., 1966, Review of Lüddekins, Ägyptishe Eheverträge. *Journal of Near Eastern Studies,* 25:135–36.

JETT, STEPHEN C., 1962, "Pueblo Indian Migration: An Evaluation of the Possible Physical and Cultural Determinants." *American Antiquity,* 29:281–300.

KAISER, WERNER, 1956, "Stand und Probleme der ägyptische Vorgeschichtsforschung." *Zeitschrift fur ägyptische Sprache und Altertumskunde,* 81:87–109.

———, 1957, Zur Inneren Chronologie der Naqadakultur." *Archaeologia Geographica,* 6:69–78.

KANTOR, HELENE J., 1965, "The Relative Chronology of Egypt and its Foreign Correlations before the Late Bronze Age." Robert W. Ehrich (ed.), *Chronologies in Old World Archaeology.* Chicago: University of Chicago Press, pp. 1–46.

KEES, HERMANN, 1961, *Ancient Egypt: A Cultural Topography.* Chicago: University of Chicago Press.

KENYON, KATHLEEN, 1960, *Archaeology in the Holy Land.* London: Ernest Benn, Ltd.

———, 1961, *Beginning in Archaeology.* London: Phoenix House.

KLUCKHOHN, CLYDE, 1936, "Some Reflections on the Method and Theory of the Kulturkreislehre." *American Anthropologist,* 38:157–196.

———, 1962, *Culture and Behavior: Collected Essays of Clyde Kluckhohn.* New York: The Free Press.

KRAELING, CARL H., and ROBERT M. ADAMS, 1960, *City Invincible: a Symposium on Urbanization and Cultural Development in the Ancient Near East.* Chicago: University of Chicago Press.

KROEBER, ALFRED L., 1925, Handbook of the Indians of California. *Bureau of American Ethnology,* Bulletin 78.

———, 1931, "The Culture-area and Age-area Concepts of Clark Wissler." S. A. Rice (ed.) *Methods in Social Science.* Chicago: University of Chicago Press, pp. 248–265.

———, 1940, "Stimulus Diffusion." *American Anthropologist,* 42:1–20.

————, 1948, *Anthropology*, new ed. New York: Harcourt, Brace & World, Inc.

————, 1953, "The Delimitation of Civilizations." *Journal of the History of Ideas*, 14:264–275.

LAMBDIN, THOMAS O., 1961, "Egypt: Its Language and Literature." G. Ernest Wright (ed.), *The Bible and the Ancient Near East.* New York: Doubleday and Company, Inc., pp. 279–297.

LEACH, EDMUND, 1954, *The Political Systems of Highland Burma.* Cambridge, Mass.: Harvard University Press.

————, 1960, "The Frontiers of Burma." *Comparative Studies in Society and History*, 3:49–68.

————, 1961*a*, *Pul Eliya: a Village in Ceylon.* Cambridge, England: Cambridge University Press.

————, 1961*b*, *Rethinking Anthropology.* London School of Economics, Monographs on Social Anthropology, No. 22.

LÉVI-STRAUSS, CLAUDE, 1953, "Social Structure." A. L. Kroeber, *Anthropology Today.* Chicago: University of Chicago Press, pp. 524–553.

————, 1963, *Structural Anthropology.* New York: Basic Books, Inc.

LEWIS, HERBERT S., n.d., "Ethnology and African Culture-History." Paper to be published in the Northwestern Univ. Program of African Studies Symposium on African Culture History.

————, 1966, "The Origins of the Galla and Somali." *Journal of African History*, 7:27–46.

LINTON, RALPH, 1933. The Tanala. Field Museum of Natural History. *Anthropological Series*, 21:1–334.

————, 1936, *The Study of Man.* New York: Appleton-Century-Crofts.

LIVINGSTONE, FRANK B., 1958, "Anthropological Implications of Sickle Cell Gene Distribution in West Africa." *American Anthropologist*, 60:533–562.

LONGACRE, WILLIAM A., 1964, "Archaeology as Anthropology: a case study:" *Science*, 144:1454–1455.

————, 1966, "Changing Patterns of Social Integration: a Prehistoric Example from the American Southwest." *American Anthropologist*, 68:94–102.

LOUNSBURY, FLOYD G., 1961, "Iroquois-Cherokee Linguistic Relations." William N. Fenton and John Gulick (eds.), Symposium on Cherokee and Iroquois Culture. Smithsonian Institution: *Bureau of American Ethnology*, Bulletin 180, pp. 11–17.

LOWIE, ROBERT H., 1912, "On the Principle of Convergence in Ethnology." *Journal of American Folklore*, 25:24–42.

————, 1918, "Survivals and Historical Method." *American Journal of Sociology*, 23:529–535.

————, 1927, *The Origin of the State.* New York: Harcourt, Brace & World, Inc.

————, 1937, *The History of Ethnological Theory.* New York: Holt, Rinehart and Winston, Inc.

————, 1960, "Some Problems of Geographical Distribution." Cora DuBois (ed.), *Lowie's Selected Papers in Anthropology.* Berkeley and Los Angeles: University of California Press, pp. 441–460.

LOWTHER, GORDON R., 1962, "Epistemology and Archaeological Theory." *Current Anthropology*, 3:495–509.

McBURNEY, C. B. M., 1960, *The Stone Age of Northern Africa.* Baltimore: Penguin Books, Inc.

McCALL, DANIEL F., 1964, *Africa in Time-Perspective: a Discussion of Historical Reconstruction from Unwritten Sources.* Boston: Boston University Press.

MacGAFFEY, WYATT, 1966, "Concepts of Race in the Historiography of Northeast Africa." *Journal of African History*, 7:1–17.

MacLEOD, WILLIAM C., 1924, The Origin of the State Reconsidered in the Light of Aboriginal North America. Philadelphia: University of Pennsylvania Thesis.

102 · GENERAL BIBLIOGRAPHY

MacNeish, Richard S., 1952, Iroquois Pottery Types: a Technique for the Study of Iroquois Prehistory. Ottawa: National Museum of Canada, Bulletin No. 124.

MacWhite, Eoin, 1956, "On the Interpretation of Archaeological Evidence in Historical and Sociological Terms." *American Anthropologist,* 58:3–25.

Martin, Paul S., George I. Quimby and Donald Collier, 1947, *Indians Before Columbus: Twenty Thousand Years of North American History Revealed by Archeology.* Chicago: University of Chicago Press.

Meggers, Betty J., 1964. "North and South American Cultural Connections and Convergences." In Jesse D. Jennings and Edward Norbeck (eds.), *Prehistoric Man in the New World.* Chicago: University of Chicago Press, pp. 511–526.

Moore, Harvey C., 1954, "Cumulation and Cultural Process." *American Anthropologist,* 56:347–357.

Moore, Stanley, 1960, "Marxian Theories of Law in Primitive Society." Stanley Diamond (ed.), *Culture in History Essays in Honor of Paul Radin.* New York: Columbia University Press, pp. 642–662.

Morgan, Lewis Henry, 1871, Systems of Consanguinity and Affinity of the Human Family. *Smithsonian Institution Contributions to Knowledge 17,* No. 218.

———, 1907, *Ancient Society.* Chicago: Chas. Kerr (originally printed 1877).

Murdock, George Peter, 1945, "The Common Denominator of Cultures." Ralph Linton (ed.), *The Science of Man in the World Crisis.* New York: Columbia University Press, pp. 122–142.

———, 1949, *Social Structure.* New York: The Macmillian Coupany.

———, 1959a, *Africa, Its Peoples and their Culture History.* New York: McGraw-Hill Book Company, Inc.

———, 1959b, "Cross-language Parallels in Parental Kin Terms." *Anthropological Linguistics,* 1:9:1–5.

———, 1959c, "Evolution in Social Organization." Betty J. Meggers, (ed.), *Evolution and Anthropology: a Centennial Appraisal.* The Anthropological Society of Washington, pp. 126–143.

Murray, Margaret A., 1951, *The Splendour that was Egypt.* London: Sidgwick & Jackson, Ltd.

———, 1956, "Burial Customs and Beliefs in the Hereafter in PreDynastic Egypt" *Journal of Egyptian Archaeology,* 42:86–96.

Nadel, Siegfried F., 1951, *The Foundations of Social Anthropology.* New York: The Free Press.

Nagel, Ernest, 1961, *The Structure of Science: Problems in the Logic of Scientific Explanation.* New York: Harcourt, Brace & World, Inc.

Nelson, Nels C., 1919, "The Archaeology of the Southwest: a Preliminary Report." *Proceedings of the National Academy of Sciences,* Vol. 5, pp. 114–210.

Neustupny, Euzen and Jiri, 1961, *Czechoslovakia before the Slavs.* London: Thames and Hudson.

Nims, Charles M., 1965, *Thebes of the Pharaohs.* London: Elek Books Ltd.

Oppenheimer, Franz, 1914, *The State.* Indianapolis: The Bobbs-Merrill Company, Inc.

Palmer, Leonard R., 1965, *Mycenaeans and Minoans: Aegean Prehistory in the Light of Linear B Tablets.* London: Faber & Faber, Ltd. (2nd edition).

Parker, Arthur C., 1916, "The Origin of the Iroquois as Suggested by their Archaeology." *American Anthropologist,* 18:479–507.

Passarge, Siegfried, 1940, Die Urlandschaft Ägyptens und die Lokalisierung der Wiege der altägyptischen Kultur. *Nova Acta Leopoldina,* 9:77–152.

Perry, William J., 1923, *The Children of the Sun.* London: Methuen & Company, Ltd.

Petrie, William M. F., 1901, *Diospolis Parva.* London: Egypt Exploration Fund Memoirs, No. 20.

———, 1939, *The Making of Egypt.* London: Sheldon Press.

PIGGOTT, STUART, 1959, *Approach to Archaeology*. Cambridge, Mass.: Harvard University Press.

———, 1961, *The Dawn of Civilization*. New York: McGraw-Hill Book Company, Inc.

———, 1965, *Ancient Europe from the Beginnings of Agriculture to Classical Antiquity*. Chicago: Aldine Publishing Company.

POPE, MAURICE, 1966, The Origins of Writing in the Near East. *Antiquity*, 40:17–23.

POSPISIL, LEOPOLD, 1958, "Social Change and Primitive Law: Consequences of a Papuan Legal Case." *American Anthropologist*, 60:832–837.

POWELL, T. G. E., 1958, *The Celts*. London: Thames and Hudson.

RADCLIFFE-BROWN, ALFRED R., 1957, *A Natural Science of Society*. New York: The Free Press.

———, 1958 (M. N. Srinivas, ed.), *Method in Social Anthropology*. Chicago: University of Chicago Press.

RAGLAN, FITZ ROY, R. S., 1939, *How Came Civilization?* London: Methuen & Co., Ltd.

RANDS, ROBERT L., 1953, "The Water Lily in Maya Art: a Complex of Alleged Asiatic Origin." *Bureau of American Ethnology*, Bulletin 151:75–154.

———, 1956, "Comparative Notes on the Hand-eye and Related Motifs." *American Antiquity*, 22:247–257.

———, 1961, "Elaboration and Invention in Ceramic Tradition." *American Antiquity*, 26:331–341.

RANDS, ROBERT L. AND C. L. RILEY, 1958, "Diffusion and Discontinuous Distribution." *American Anthropologist* 60:274–297.

REDFIELD, ROBERT, 1941, *The Folk Culture of Yucatan*. Chicago: University of Chicago Press.

———, 1947, "The Folk Society." *American Journal of Sociology*, 52:293–308.

REED, CHARLES A., 1960, "A Review of the Archaeological Evidence on Animal Domestication in the Prehistoric Near East." Robert J. Braidwood and Bruce Howe (eds.), *Prehistoric Investigations in Iraqi Kurdistan*. Chicago: University of Chicago Press, pp. 119–145.

RILEY, CARROLL, L., 1952, "The Blowgun in the New World." *Southwestern Journal of Anthropology*, 8:297–319.

ROGERS, EVERETT M., 1962, *Diffusion of Innovations*. New York: The Free Press.

ROUSE, IRVING, 1953, "The Strategy of Culture History." A. L. Kroeber (ed.), *Anthropology Today*. Chicago: University of Chicago Press, pp. 57–76.

———, 1958, "The Inference of Migrations from Anthropological Evidence." Raymond H. Thompson (ed.), *Migrations in New World Culture History*. Tucson, Ariz.: University of Arizona, Social Science Bulletin, No. 27, pp. 63–68.

———, 1960, "The Classification of Artifacts in Archaeology." *American Antiquity*, 25:313–323.

———, 1964, "Prehistory of the West Indies." *Science*, 144: 499–513.

———, 1965, "The Place of 'Peoples' in Prehistoric Research." *Journal of the Royal Anthropological Institute*, 95:1–15.

ROWE, JOHN HOWLAND, 1966, "Diffusionism and Archaeology." *American Antiquity*, 31:334–337.

SANDERS, WILLIAM T., 1965, The Cultural Ecology of the Teotihuacan Valley. *A Preliminary Report of the Results of the Teotihuacan Valley Project*. Department of Sociology and Anthropology, The Pennsylvania State University.

SAPIR, EDWARD, 1916, Time Perspective in Aboriginal American Culture. Canada Department of Mines, Memoir, No. 90.

———, 1921, *Language, an Introduction to the Study of Speech*. New York: Harcourt, Brace & World, Inc.

SCHMIDT, WILHELM, 1939, *The Culture Historical Method of Ethnology*, trans. S. A. Sieber, New York: Fortuny's.

SCHROEDER, ALBERT H., 1964, "Unregulated Diffusion from Mexico into the Southwest Prior to A.D. 700." *American Antiquity*, 30:297–307.

SEARS, WILLIAM H., 1961, "The Study of Social and Religious Systems in North American Archaeology." *Current Anthropology*, 2:223–246.

SEBAG, LUCIEN, 1964, *Marxisme et Structuralisme*. Paris: Payot.

SELIGMAN, CHARLES G. and MARGARET A. MURRAY, 1911, "Note Upon an Early Egyptian Standard." *Man*, 11:165–171.

SEMENOV, S. A., 1964, *Prehistoric Technology: an Experimental Study of the Oldest Tools and Artifacts from Traces of Manufacture and Wear*. London: Cory, Adams and MacKay.

SERVICE, ELMAN R., 1964, "Archaeological Theory and Ethnological Fact." Robert A. Manners (ed.), *Process and Pattern in Culture*. Chicago: Aldine Publishing Company, pp. 364–375.

SHARP, ANDREW, 1957, *Ancient Voyagers in the South Pacific*. Baltimore, Md.: Penguin Books, Inc.

SJOBERG, GIDEON, 1960, *The Preindustrial City*. New York: The Free Press.

SMITH, GRAFTON ELLIOT, 1915, *The Migrations of Early Culture*. Manchester: Manchester University Press.

———, 1924, *Elephants and Ethnologists*. New York: E. P. Dutton & Com., Inc.

SMITH, HARRY S., 1964, "Egypt and C¹⁴ Dating." *Antiquity*, 38:32–37.

SMITH, WILLIAM STEVENSON, 1958, *The Art & Architecture of Ancient Egypt*. Baltimore: Penguin Books.

SONNENFELD, J., 1962, "Interpreting the Function of Primitive Implements." *American Antiquity*, 28:56–65.

SPIER, LESLIE, 1921, The Sun Dance of the Plains Indians: Its Development and Diffusion. American Museum of Natural History, *Anthropological Papers*, 16:7.

STENBERGER, MARTEN, n.d., *Sweden*. London: Thames and Hudson.

STEWARD, JULIAN H., 1929, "Diffusion and Independent Development: a Critique of Logic." *American Anthropologist*, 31:491–495.

———, 1942, "The Direct Historical Approach to Archaeology." *American Antiquity*, 7:337–343.

———, 1955, *Theory of Cultural Change*. Urbana, Ill.: University of Illinois Press.

———, 1960, "Some Implications of the Symposium." Julian Steward, *et al.*, *Irrigation Civilizations: A Comparative Study*. Washington, D.C.: Pan American Union, Social Science Monographs 1, pp. 58–78.

STEWARD, JULIAN H. and F. M. SETZLER, 1938, "Function and Configuration in Archaeology." *American Antiquity*, 4:4–10.

STURTEVANT, WILLIAM, C., 1960, The Significance of Ethnological Similarities Between Southeastern North America and the Antilles. New Haven, Conn.: *Yale University Publications in Anthropology*, No. 64.

SUGGS, ROBERT C., 1960, *The Island Civilizations of Polynesia*. New York: Mentor Books, New American Library.

TALLGREN, A. M., 1937, "The Method of Prehistoric Archaeology." *Antiquity*, 11:152–161.

TAYLOR, WALTER W. JR., 1948, A Study of Archaeology. *Memoirs of the American Anthropological Association*, No. 69.

TAYLOR, WILLIAM E. JR., 1966, "An Archaeological Perspective on Eskimo Economy." *Antiquity*, 40:114–120.

THIEME, PAUL, 1964, "The Comparative Method for Reconstruction in Linguistics." Dell Hymes (ed.) *Language in Culture and Society*. New York: Harper & Row, Publishers, pp. 585–598.

THOMPSON, RAYMOND H., 1958, Migrations in New World Culture History. Tucson: University of Arizona: *Social Science Bulletin*, No. 27.

TOLSTOY, PAUL, 1953, "Some Amerasian Pottery Traits in North Asian Prehistory." *American Antiquity*, 19:25–40.

TRIGGER, BRUCE G., 1965, History and Settlement in Lower Nubia. New Haven, Conn.: *Yale University Publications in Anthropology*, No. 69.

————, 1966*a*, "The Languages of the Northern Sudan: an Historical Perspective." *Journal of African History*, 7:19–25.

————, 1966*b*, "Sir Daniel Wilson: Canada's First Anthropologist." *Anthropologica*, 8:1–28.

TYLOR, EDWARD B., 1879, "On the Game of Patolli in Ancient Mexico and its Probably Asiatic Origin." *Journal of the Royal Anthropological Institute*, 8:116–129.

————, 1889, "On a Method of Investigation of the Development of Institutions, Applied to Laws of Marriage and Descent." *Journal of the Royal Anthropological Institute*, 18:245–269.

VANDIER, JACQUES, 1952, Manuel d'Archéologie Egyptienne, Vol. I. *Les époques de formation: la préhistoire*. Paris: Edition A. et J. Picard et Cie.

VANSINA, JAN, 1965, *Oral Tradition: a Study in Historical Methodology*. Chicago: Aldine Publishing Company.

WALLACE, ANTHONY F. C., 1961, *Culture and Personality*. New York: Random House, Inc.

WEBER, MAX, 1958, *The City*. New York: The Free Press.

WHEELER, ROBERT E. M., 1954, *Archaeology from the Earth*. Oxford: Clarendon Press.

WHITE, LESLIE, 1949, *The Science of Culture*. New York: Grove Press, Inc.

WILLEY, GORDON R., 1953*a*, "A Pattern of Diffusion-Acculturation." *Southwestern Journal of Anthropology* 9:369–384.

————, 1953*b*, "Archaeological Theories and Interpretation: New World." A. L. Kroeber (ed.), *Anthropology Today*. Chicago: University of Chicago Press, pp. 361–385.

WILLEY, GORDON R. and PHILIP PHILLIPS, 1958, *Method and Theory in American Archaeology*. Chicago: University of Chicago Press.

WILSON, DANIEL, 1851, *The Archaeology and Prehistoric Annals of Scotland*. London: MacMillan & Company, Ltd.

WISSLER, CLARK, 1917, *The American Indian*. New York: McMurtrie.

————, 1923, *Man and Culture*. New York: Thomas Y. Corwell Company.

————, 1927, *The Relation of Nature to Man in Aboriginal America*. London: Oxford University Press.

WITTFOGEL, KARL A., 1957, *Oriental Despotism: a Comparative Study of Total Power*. New Haven, Conn.: Yale University Press.

————, 1959, "The Theory of Oriental Society." Morton H. Fried (ed.), *Readings in Anthropology*, Vol. 2. New York: Thomas Y. Crowell Company, pp. 94–113.

WOLF, ERIC, 1951, "The Social Organization of Mecca and the Origins of Islam." *Southwestern Journal of Anthropology*, 7: 329–355.

WRIGHT, JAMES V., 1965, "A Regional Examination of Ojibwa Culture History." *Anthropologica*, 7:189–227.

YEIVIN, SAMUEL, 1965, "Some Remarks on the Early Protodynastic Period." Paper read at the Annual Meeting of the American Research Center in Egypt, 1965.

ZUIDEMA, R. T., 1964, *The Ceque System of Cuzco*. Leiden: Brill.